M000209484

CONNECTING THROUGH "YES!"

How to Agree When You Don't Agree to Get Cooperation and Closeness in Your Marriage

JACK ITO, PH.D.

Loving Solutions Publishing • Kingsport, Tennessee

CONNECTING THROUGH "YES!"
How to Agree When You Don't Agree to Get Cooperation and Closeness in Your Marriage
by Jack Ito

Published by:
Loving Solutions Publishing
Suite F30
1000 University Boulevard
Kingsport, TN 37660 USA
orders@lovingsolutionspublishing.com

Unattributed quotations are by Jack Ito

ISBN, print ed.   978-0-9890999-1-2

Library of Congress Control Number: 2013905791

DEDICATION

This book is dedicated to my wife, Toshie. Thank you for loving me more than needing me. Thank you for being a true partner who helps me to develop myself in our marriage. While it has not always been easy, it has always been worth it.

CONTENTS

WARNING—DISCLAIMER

This book was written to provide general guidance for improving communication and reducing conflict. It was not written to provide interventions for people at risk of physical harm. It also is not a substitute for treatment of a psychological disorder. Any persons needing assistance with such situations should consult professional help, including psychological, psychiatric, supportive, and legal services.

A good relationship does not happen quickly. Anyone who decides to have a good long term relationship must work on it continuously, both addressing concerns and promoting positive communication. This book addresses an important aspect of communication. It can't be used as a comprehensive manual on communication or relating. No book could conceivably offer all that is needed to guarantee a positive long term relationship. Human interaction is simply too complex.

Great care has been taken to make this book as complete and accurate as possible regarding its content. However, there *may be mistakes*, both typographical and in content. Therefore this book should be used only as a general guide and not as the ultimate source of managing relational differences. Furthermore, this book is current only up until the printing date.

In a book of this sort, it is not possible to take into account individual differences that influence the success or failure of these methods. The author and publisher have no responsibility to any person or entity in regard to loss or damage caused, or thought to have been caused, directly or indirectly by the contents of this book.

If you are not in agreement with this disclaimer, you may return the book to the seller for a full refund.

INTRODUCTION

The Methods You Use Determine the Results You Get

Most marriages and other relationships can be saved when people use loving and effective methods to deal with problems. These methods are available to everyone, but known by few. This book teaches these methods. This book is different from others in that it starts at the point of conflict and teaches you how to improve a relationship with an uncooperative spouse or partner. The examples are practical and real. They are drawn from 20 years of coaching and counseling.

Most people don't even know the basics about building a marriage. They marry with the expectation that serious problems won't happen. When they do, they are unprepared, shocked and angered. They do and say things that damage rather than mend. They live with the daily frustration of wanting to be closer, but not being able to. They become more distant the more they try to fix things. Eventually, they give up trying and begin waiting. They can spend years of their life waiting for they don't even know what. While they wait, problems accumulate until their love is burned out or their spouse is gone. By waiting too long to learn how to effectively deal with their problems, they become another divorce statistic.

The reason people need effective methods for dealing with problems however, is not to lower the divorce rate. Who cares about the divorce rate? It's just statistics. What people care about is what happens to *them*. They don't want to feel lonely, hurt, frustrated, angry, or worried for the rest of their lives. If divorce can end that pain, they will do it eventually. Unfortunately, because of ineffective methods of problem solving, divorce has become the third most popular method for dealing with hurtful differences. The two most popular methods, equally ineffective, are arguing and avoidance. Couples argue in an effort to fix their problems. When that doesn't work, they start to avoid each other. This leads eventually to divorce. To prevent divorce, we need to exchange the first method—arguing—for something better. Then avoidance will never be necessary and love can be renewed.

Looking for a New (*and Better*) Way to Handle Relationship Problems

A new model for loving relationships needs to help couples to talk about differences *no matter* what those differences are. Couples need to be able to talk about small things such as which way the toilet paper should unroll, and big things like temptations to have an affair. Using their current skills, very few couples would be able to talk about being tempted to have an affair. Because couples can't talk about such things, problems are not prevented and opportunities for connection are lost. Every one of us has internal struggles. Having someone to share them with is an important part of a healthy marriage. Isn't this one of the reasons that we get married in the first place? Do we really have to wait until the muck hits the fan before we can talk about things? Waiting to get to that point before we talk is likely to make problems worse rather than better.

The reality is that most people don't realize they need a new way of talking until they are already in the thick of things. They are surprised by the hateful things they say to each other, and they conclude that their love must be forever gone. In my work as a marriage and relationship coach, I never get contacted by couples who tell me that they want to learn to communicate well so that they don't develop major problems. I only hear from them *after* the major problems have already developed. Fortunately, with the right help, even then is not too late.

My calling is to help people save relationships and love each other. Because of that, I use methods that help people to emotionally reconnect, even after a lot of damage has been done. Those methods do *not* involve argument or avoidance.

In real life, bad things happen. Affairs, criticizing and blaming, emotional abuse, physical abuse, financial debts, psychological disorders, conflicts about parenting, and physical illness are only a sampling of what can go wrong. It is only a matter of time before something bad happens in a relationship. The way those events are handled are better predictors of the relationship continuing than the events themselves.

How can couples begin to address such issues in their relationships? If any of these things happened in your relationship, which ones would you be able to *lovingly and effectively* talk about with your spouse? Few couples are prepared to manage such problems in a way that preserves their love and the relationship. Instead, couples live in the hope that things like that will never happen. When they do, they feel sick to their stomach and have no idea of where to begin.

Divorce Is an Answer, Just Not a Good One

Currently, couples with such problems are frequently recommended, by well intentioned friends and family, as well as others, to separate or divorce. Incredibly, there are even marriage counselors and coaches who recommend divorce. I am not one of them. If divorce actually solved problems, divorcing might be a good recommendation. But, divorce as a "method" for happiness is flawed. Divorce is at best an emotional amputation and not a method of healing. It always results in loss, and the pain of it is often experienced long into the future. What's more, one divorce impacts multiple generations.

What many of us have learned from our parents, and are unintentionally teaching to our children, is when we have major differences with our spouse, we *should* be angry, defend ourselves, and insist that we are right. We have not learned to connect in the midst of our differences and to support and love each other even as we are working things out. That way seems like something from a time long ago.

When I married my wife, I committed to love her. But, I wasn't naïve enough to believe that the intentions we had on our wedding day would be enough to carry us lovingly through the years. Because, as a veteran marriage and relationship coach, I know that every relationship will have difficulty sooner or later.

Some people who realize that problems eventually occur in every relationship think it better not to marry at all but to live together instead. Avoiding a marital commitment does not help to avoid problems because the problems are not caused by marriage. Avoiding marriage just results in cheap commitment and disposable relationships.

Work on Love and the Marriage Will Take Care of Itself

I believe there is a danger in seeing marriage as a legal contract which culminates in a wedding ceremony. For my wife and I, and for many other couples, we would rather sacrifice our legal status than sacrifice our love for each other. Love is the fundamental thing. Love is at the heart of what relationships are all about. Love is the reason we have relationships in the first place. The marriage *ceremony* is the social, legal, and public expression of a loving commitment, much as a birth certificate is for the parents of a newborn. *Marriage* though, is a description of the ongoing loving relationship between husband and wife. When that stops, the marriage has stopped also. Saving marriages is about keeping the love going more than it is about preventing divorce.

My commitment is to my wife, *not* to my marriage. While it may seem like splitting hairs, it makes things really clear when problems arise. Instead of saying, "How can I save my marriage?"

I say, "How can I best love my wife in this situation?" And, because my commitment is to her, she is far less likely to need secrets, to hesitate to talk to me, or to want to avoid me. Take care of the relationship, and the marriage takes care of itself.

What's Your Method?

Everyone has a way of dealing with differences, although they don't think of it as their "method." That's what it is though. The methods that most people use to deal with differences actually turn *mere differences* into *irreconcilable differences.* The process goes something like this: small differences create an emotional disconnect; then, like a snowball, this disconnect accumulates more and more disconnects. When the accumulated differences get too great, the relationship cannot take the strain, and breaks under the pressure—just as a giant snowball would.

If a couple has a difference of opinion about something, what methods are open to them to resolve their differences? We can consider this in terms of both small and large differences. Take a difference as small as deciding which way to hang the toilet paper roll. Should it unroll from the front or the back? And how about a larger issue like how to spend the income? And perhaps an even larger difference like one spouse having an affair?

These are the commonly used methods couples use to resolve such differences:
1. Debate/Argument/Convincing
2. Authority
3. Power/Threat
4. Avoidance
5. Asking

Debate/Argument/Convincing

Debate is a commonly used method in Western countries which value an equality between the sexes. In a debate, each person presents their viewpoint along with reasoning, examples, and evidence, if they have any. Simultaneously, they try to discredit their partner's position. Because there is no judge in these one on one debates, there is no way of actually deciding a winner. Instead, each person becomes more convinced by his or her own ideas; the more forcefully they are argued, the more difficult they are to give up.

Not only is impartiality a problem in debate, but unfair tactics are also used. One such tactic, which is very primitive, is being loud. The monkey which screeches the loudest may win simply because the other monkeys are afraid of his or her going berserk. For people who have partners that do the screeching monkey, they will know exactly what I am talking about.

Yet another unfair tactic in debate is bringing in unrelated arguments. When I argue with you, I can remind you of all the poor decisions you made in the past and how they led to a great number of problems. In marriage counseling jargon, this is known as bringing out the laundry list. You, as my debate partner, can then defend and argue about those additional issues from the past, bring in your own laundry list to use against me, or do the screeching monkey to try to shut me up. If I were losing the debate, that may have been the goal that I was really hoping for—shutting you up. I will have had an emotional victory simply by preventing you from winning.

If the debate goes on too long, I may decide that it's not worth my energy to continue to debate about it and withdraw. Even if my partner wants to continue to debate, I won't participate and the debate will come to an end. That can take a while as each person usually likes to be the one to get in the last word. Then, our debate may resume on another day, or if it is a small matter (like the toilet paper roll), it may be added to the list of things that we can never talk about again.

One more possible way of ending a debate is for one person to surrender (give-in). This does not happen by one person saying, "Wow, what you have said really makes sense. I'm sorry I argued about it. Let's do it your way." Instead, it typically is reflected by some kind of strained agreement, underlying resentment, and possibly with tearfulness. If one's partner is sensitive enough, the tears can even be used as an additional tactic to win the debate. Such a tactic becomes less and less effective the more it's used, however.

Although couples don't think of this as a *method* that they repeatedly employ when they have problems, nevertheless, a method it is. And, an ineffective and damaging one at that.

Authority

Yet another method open to couples who have differences large and small is *authority*. In some Western countries and in many Eastern ones, one member of the family is vested with the power to make the final decision. Often, it is the husband, the master of his house, the king of his castle. Other times it is the father, mother, or mother-in-law (gasp). Authority can also be extended outside the family such as to a priest or pastor, or to a marriage counselor.

Regardless of the source of the authority, unless both the husband and wife respect the authority, it won't settle anything. However, in cases where they both respect the line of authority, it avoids the pitfalls common with debate such as the screeching monkey, laundry list, and unhappy surrender. Withdrawing though, is still likely to happen, if not on the physical level then at least on an emotional one. Compliance with authority, does not ensure *emotional* consent. For relationships that depend on love to hold them together, authority typically fails.

Power/Threat

So, what else are couples left with if they don't debate, and don't have the decision of an authority? Well, there is always *threat*. Physical threats include those of bodily injury as well as threats to stop funding food, shelter, or other physical welfare kinds of aid. When a country withholds aid from another country that needs it, you know which country has more power. There is more than one way to beat someone into submission.

Psychological power is far more common and is particularly easy to use against a needy partner. Although everyone has a fear of abandonment or rejection, often one partner feels it more keenly. Sometimes one partner merely has to use a certain look or tone of voice to set the other partner's insecurities trembling.

Physical and psychological power results in forced compliance and *compiling resentments.* If it weren't for the outlet of divorce and police protection, the murder rate would be much higher among spouses, mainly because of the misuse of physical and psychological power. According to the US Department of Justice, nearly 1 of every 5 murders happens in intimate relationships, with wives and girlfriends being twice at risk as husbands and boyfriends.[1]

Clearly, debate, authority, and power are not good solutions for handling any of our differences, big or small. Whether our differences are about how to hang the toilet paper roll, spend our money, or deal with a spouse who is having an affair, debate, authority, and power fail to build our relationships. They can result in a decision being made, but always at a cost to the relationship. The price is paid out of the reservoir of love that we have to start with. And, if the problems are big or frequent, our reservoirs of love dry up. Many of my clients tell me their "container is empty." They have given too much, for too long, while getting too little in return.

Avoidance

One other option open to people is not really a method for resolving problems at all, although it is frequently used when problems arise. It is the method of *avoidance.* Avoidance means that I see the problem, but am choosing not to do anything about it. I am likely to make that choice because I believe that trying to do something about it will create an even bigger problem.

People who use avoidance have usually learned to do that through experience in their current relationship, in a past one, or in their families of origin. An easily recognizable pattern in relationships with no good method of resolving differences is: 1)

---

[1] US Department of Justice, Bureau of Justice Statistics. *Homicide Trends in the United States, 1980-2008.* Retrieved from BJS website: http://bjs.ojp.usdoj.gov/content/pub/pdf/htus8008.pdf on November 28, 2012.

initial closeness, followed by 2) petty arguments, followed by 3) major arguments, followed by 4) avoidance, and then eventually 5) rejection and abandonment. Each of these stages is predictable. Knowing which stage you are in now will help you know what is going to happen next unless positive changes are made.

Faced with relationship problems, which of these methods could you effectively use to create positive change?

Debate
Authority
Power
Avoidance

It's hard to believe that any of these will result in positive change. And, if not these, then what else? I can think of a few more things people often try, including asking, begging, whining, and nagging. Begging, whining, and nagging sometimes result in temporary change, but do long term damage.

Asking, the Underused Method

Asking actually works pretty well in close relationships, but for some reason not a lot of people use it. When I work with husbands or wives who complain about their spouse not responding in a certain way or doing a certain thing, I check to see if they have ever clearly asked for what they want. Much of the time, they haven't.

For example, a wife might say to me that whenever she wants her husband to listen and be sensitive to her feelings, he interrupts and starts giving solutions. Then, when I ask her if she has tried asking him to just listen without interrupting until she has finished, she says that she never has. It has never occurred to her to ask. Likely she has complained about his not listening, or his interrupting, but that's not the same as asking him to listen without interrupting. When the women I work with try that, they find that in most cases it works.

It makes me wonder why being adversarial comes so naturally, while asking seems so hard—even with people who have promised us their undying love. The only answer I have come up with for that is that people do what they know how to do and what has worked for them in the past, no matter how little it has worked. Most people have little experience with asking and more experience with complaining, so they naturally complain more.

A New Method to Replace the Ones That Don't Really Work

This book presents an alternative which on the surface sounds very controversial, but which has more promise for resolving problems and building relationships than any of the other methods. This method is already in use in some counseling offices and in places where getting along really matters, such as between heads of state.

Simply stated, this alternative method is using *agreement* as much as possible to achieve a different goal—a win-win. The old goal of one-sided *winning* (also known as *being right*) does not work with agreement. Win-win is not concerned with being right. Win-win is concerned with *connection*, *cooperation*, and *growth*. Whereas debate and seeking to be right leads to disconnection, distancing, and stagnation, agreement leads in the other direction.

The method of agreement is not a new tweak, or a new twist. It's an altogether different approach. It seems radical only because recently people have moved away from the traditional goals of love and commitment toward a new standard of convenience and individuality. Quite frankly, this new way saddens me. It shakes the very foundation of my belief that we are beings created in God's image with a primary purpose of loving Him and one another. Agreement is not an evolutionary model. It is not based on survival of the fittest. No doubt many people will find it as misguided as I do the debate model.

Although agreement is not about winning, it is not about surrender either. It has nothing to do with rolling on your back and exposing your neck. If anything, agreement levels the playing field. Debate is a method of domination through intellect. Agreement is a method of support and partnership. Agreement is not acquiescence. It does not say, "If you want to hurt me, I agree with you." Doing that would not be loving any more than whacking someone up beside the head with a frying pan. Both of these actions will destroy a relationship. If that is what agreement was about, I would write a book about how to win a debate instead. I have no desire to see anyone hurt.

Example: The president and the foreign leader

So how does agreement work then? Well, let's take a look at a modern day example of how agreement is used in a political context. The president of the USA invites a foreign leader or two to the USA, perhaps to Camp David. Let's say that country's leader wants to do something that the US president finds appalling, like testing nuclear weapons. Although that might not seem as big to you as your spouse having an affair, trust me, it's a big issue with the potential to do a lot of damage. But, if you prefer, you can imagine saving the whales from extinction (another worthy cause). Anyway, do you think the first thing that's going to happen when the president meets the foreign leader at the airport is for the president to say, "What the hell were you thinking?" He might like to say that, *feel* like saying that, but that would not be productive. If the president did that, the foreign leader would turn around and go home and the relationship of our two countries would be worse than ever.

So, what does he do instead? He asks about the flight, offers the foreign leader coffee, talks about the weather, or sports, or something light. The message at first meeting is "You are welcome here. I want us to have a good time and talk together in a way that won't stress either of us out." This is the first part of the agreement model—setting the stage for cooperation by being nice. By being considerate. By realizing that there are two human beings here, each with legitimate needs, and not just one.

Now, do you think the next thing the president is going to do is threaten to cut off all aid and trade to that foreign country unless that leader makes some drastic changes to his or her thinking right away? No way, Americans are sick of war. The president wouldn't gain anything in provoking one. It might rather go something like this, "I understand that you want your country to be one of the world leaders. To be strong financially, and to not be intimidated by other countries. I think that is a fine goal." Has the president said, "Yeah, if I were you, I would test all the bombs I could?" No. Remember, agreement never seeks to damage the relationship and that is what that kind of thing would do.

Example: The wife and the unfaithful husband

To bring it a little closer to home, what about the woman whose husband is having an affair? Is she going to use agreement to tell her husband, "I agree, you should have an affair if you want to"? I sincerely hope not. But, how about this—"I can understand that you want to feel loved and valued. If I were you, I would want someone who I could feel easy with and enjoy a good sexual relationship with, too. In fact, I do want that, too." If you think she has condoned his affair, you had better reread that passage. She did nothing of the sort. Neither did she say that she wants to have an affair. What she *didn't* do is instantly jump to the punch line, "Knock it off or I'm out of here." While that is her prerogative, if she wants to save her marriage it's not a good way.

Just like the president, she is not going to stand by while her husband engages in destructive behavior, but she is not going to jump into debate and power mode. She may feel like it. Probably she will feel like doing that as well as the screeching monkey. She may need to regroup and remind herself that her husband is a human being who is trying to meet his needs more than he is trying to hurt her. And, it won't be easy. The easy thing is hurting back by rejecting him. The hard thing is loving and helping. When there is a lot at stake, that's what we must do. A couple of weeks spent agreeing and working together is worth it if it avoids years of hate and regret. And destruction. For generations.

Let's look at this from another angle. Let's suppose you were the one having the affair. Most likely you would be having it not because you were trying to think of the best way to hurt your spouse and destroy your marriage, but more likely because you were frustrated in your marriage and lonely. You are ashamed of your own behavior, but you miss so much how you used to feel, but haven't for a long time. Feeling that again helps you to feel alive. Your spouse comes to you and says one of two things. Either: 1) "I found you out, you are scum, and I'm out of here," or 2) "I know about your affair. It's something that can't go on in our marriage, but I can understand how you need to feel loved and important." Which of these two do you think is more likely to lead to reconciliation? Which one is more likely to eventually lead to your being sorry that you hurt your spouse? Things look a lot different from the other side, don't they?

Learning to Love Again

The agreement method puts "us" before "me." It requires us to think about the needs of our spouse and to consider those needs to be legitimate even if the behavior is wrong. It gives renewed meaning to love and commitment. And, it doesn't stop us from setting boundaries or even leaving the relationship if our spouse won't change. It does give the relationship the best chance to grow and succeed.

I am convinced that the agreement method is one which can replace the debate method currently in use by most couples. Although it could put a lot of lawyers and marriage counselors out of business, I feel no guilt in teaching it. My clients have been benefiting from it for years, as have I. That is all the proof I need that it works. And if you are skeptical, I won't blame you, but I challenge you to try it out for yourself. Proving me wrong through your own experience is a lot better than doing the screeching monkey, even if it is only an internal one.

No matter how well we know someone, we will never know what it is to be that person.

George Leo Robertson
from *Living is Many Things*

♥1♥

THE POWER OF AGREEMENT TO CREATE CLOSER MARRIAGES AND RELATIONSHIPS

Agreement Builds Connection

Agreement prevents defensiveness and prevents arguing. It opens your spouse's[2] mind to your perspective and helps him or her to make a more thoughtful decision. Agreement even helps to change your spouse's mind about something you don't like. *Agreement builds connection.* Agreement is a way to deal with problems without damaging your relationship.

But, how can you agree when your spouse is saying something terrible, and why would you want to? You can agree, because there is always some truth to what he or she is saying; there is always a legitimate need behind his or her behavior. And the reason why you would want to agree is because agreement creates the cooperation necessary for a close relationship.

Let's compare two approaches to the same situation:

---

[2] Throughout this book, I use "spouse" and "partner" interchangeably to mean the person you are in a a committed relationship with. I also use both "him" and "her" to intentionally emphasize both genders.

Situation: Your husband says he does not love you and wants a divorce (mentally substitute "wife" for "husband" if you are a man).

Traditional method (debate/argument):

WIFE: "What do you mean, you want a divorce?!"

HUSBAND: "Just like I said. I don't love you, I'm sick of all the bullshit and I want out. You ignore me most of the time, don't enjoy having sex anymore, and make it seem like I owe you something. And, you never make me feel like I'm good enough."

WIFE: "Me? What about you? Maybe if you paid a little attention to me, you would get more love and affection. You just expect me to always be ready for you with open arms, but you never offer to help me out. When we have sex it's 'wham, bam,' without even a 'thank you ma'am.'"

There are a thousand different things you could say using the traditional debate/argument method, but only one basic format. Each spouse will present evidence why they are right and their partner is wrong. In the process, their emotions will become more and more heated, which will make each spouse dig in his or her heels all the more. Cooperation will not be possible until one surrenders or until one is overpowered to the point that they agree on a course of action. Perhaps they will eventually agree to get counseling or to get a divorce. Whoever the loser is in this debate is not going to want to follow through, which will make the counseling less than successful or make the divorce all the more bitter.

Now, let's consider the method of agreement with the same situation.

Method of agreement:

Wife: *"What do you mean, you want a divorce?!"*

Husband: *"Just like I said. I don't love you, I'm sick of all the bullshit and I want out. You ignore me most of the time, don't enjoy having sex anymore, and make it seem like I owe you something. And, you never make me feel good enough."*

Wife: *"Wow. I guess if I didn't love you and had been frustrated for awhile, I would want a divorce, too."*

Husband: *"Yes, well, that's the way it is."*

Wife: *"Divorce is not what I want, but I certainly don't want you to be miserable in our marriage, either."*

Husband: *"Yes, well."*

Wife: *"I guess neither of us is really enjoying our marriage anymore. I'm not going to try to talk you out of divorce because I know your mind is made up."*

Husband: *"You got that right."*

Wife: *"Ok, at least let's work together on getting along until the divorce happens. There's no reason to keep fighting is there?"*

Husband: *"I guess not. We do have to get a lawyer and cooperate about things."*

Wife: *"Yes, that would be better than fighting, you're right."*

Husband: *"Now what?"*

Wife: *"I don't know. We don't have to decide how to do everything today. Let's just take a walk."*

There are many ways this can play out, too. No matter how it is played out though, it will end with the couple being able to talk and cooperate far better than with the debate method. I want you to see in this example that the wife *never* agrees with the divorce. She does not want a divorce and says so. But, she does not try to immediately change her husband's mind or to defend herself. That would only lead to debate and would solidify her husband's position against her. Instead, she starts to build a connection, which is their only hope for saving the marriage.

This is an example of a very, very, tough situation. I wanted to show you that if agreement can be used even here, to start to rebuild, it can be used with whatever other problems you are having in your relationship.

Never Agree with What Is Harmful

The goal of agreement is not to immediately solve problems or to prove your point. Neither is it to submit to your spouse and make him or her right. The goal is to calm, create connection, and cooperation. In the agreement scenario above, thanks to his wife's agreement, the husband is calming down and has already started on the path of getting along better with his wife, although he may not even realize it.

The wife has not "won" in the sense of changing her husband's mind about divorce, nor has she been needy, passive, or avoidant. She has created a win-win situation. The way she has been able to do that is by thinking about how she would feel and what she would do if she were in her husband's shoes. She could see that she might do some things differently, but that she would probably also be considering divorce and certainly not be wanting to continue a bad relationship.

I will give you many more examples of how agreement works better than debate in the remainder of this book. I am going to assume that a loving relationship is more important to you than immediately pressing and winning your point. That is the only prerequisite to using the method of agreement. If you would rather win your arguments than to calm, connect, and cooperate, then this book is not for you. It simply is not possible to focus on winning arguments and building your relationship at the same time. Don't worry though, that I'm going to ask you to give in. What I am asking is for you to be willing to create a win-win.

Agreement Calms Upset Partners

People feel angry when they are wanting someone to do something and they are not doing it. As soon as they get compliance, their anger fades away quickly. So, one way to deal with angry people is by being submissive and backing off. Although that might work well when you are not living with such a person, when that angry, upset person is your partner, being submissive and backing off is not going to end your problems. At best, it puts them off to another day, but with more resentment tacked on than the day before. What is needed is a way to calm your partner down while still maintaining good boundaries.

If someone is upset, which of these do you think would be a more calming response—"You shouldn't be upset," or "You have a right to be upset"? The fact is, as soon as you start agreeing with someone, they start to listen rather than just to argue, shout, give reasons, etc. I never teach my clients to allow themselves to be the victims of physical or verbal abuse, but I do teach them how to help their partners calm down. It's what every partner wants help with when they are upset, but don't know how to ask for.

When people are upset, they can't think straight. They say too much and overreact. They do and say things they will regret later. They hurt their partners and they hurt their relationship. When you can help your partner to calm down, you are strengthening the emotional connection, the bond, you both have. You also increase your value to your partner. If you simply submit or avoid, you lose respect, and lower your value. And, if you defend and attack, you increase the distance between you while making his or her anger worse.

What helps people to help their partners to calm down is to start with the goals of *calming, connection,* and *cooperation* rather than winning. Memorizing those three "C's" will help you to stay on track when you use the method of agreement. *Calm, Connect,* and *Cooperate.*

Agreement is Not Passive

Agreement is not at all passive. It is very active. It is mature and it is loving. Rather than just following along with what your spouse is saying, you take control of the conversation and steer it in another direction. Agreement transforms your relationship by making it easier for your spouse to come to you with sensitive issues. He or she doesn't have to hide them or attack you for having different opinions. Agreement is a leveler that keeps you and your spouse from trying to dominate each other.

Agreement Improves Problem Solving

How do you get people to cooperate with you when they have a viewpoint that is different from your own? The best way is to work on an idea that *they* came up with. If you started with *your* idea, you would have to work on proving it. With agreement, such proof is unnecessary.

For example, if you are having marital problems and you say to your spouse that you think marriage coaching would be a really good idea, you are likely to get challenged. In fact, you would need to work on presenting evidence for three things: 1) that you have significant marital problems; 2) that the marriage is worth working on; and 3) that marriage coaching is the best way to work on it.

In the process of your presenting evidence and reasons for any of these three things, you are likely to end up setting off some emotional triggers in your spouse. You will be challenged about your conception of the problems as well as your belief about what is the best way to deal with them. In short, there are a dozen ways for your spouse to intentionally or unintentionally derail you. Although you are trying to do something that would be really good, it could turn into an argument that was really bad. Has that happened to you before? Whenever we are talking to people about

6

an area where we have large differences of opinion, there is always going to be a defensive reaction (even if it is a controlled one), and often we will end up being blamed. Because of this, many people put off talking about problems until a lot of damage has been done. When you put off problems, they pile up. When the pile gets high enough, they all come crashing down like a landslide. People get hurt, and the mess is hard to clean up.

Because of the desire to avoid fighting and rejection, most people don't bring up relationship problems until the evidence is overwhelming. This is true for all conflict areas including parenting, finances, sex, dating, and the other problems described in this book. Having to wait until things are spinning out of control just so you can more easily prove that things are spinning out of control doesn't seem like the most helpful way to go about improving your relationship.

Agreement prevents the necessity of having to present a lot of evidence and multiple ideas. It prevents a defensive reaction that leads to conflict. This is because agreement is not based on selling your ideas. When you agree with someone, you don't need to present any evidence because they already believe it! If you do offer evidence why the other person is *right* or why you agree, it will be accepted at face value—"You are right, and let me tell you why…" People don't argue with you when you are proving them right.

So, if you are having problems with your marriage, how do you use agreement to get you both to the point where you are working cooperatively? First, you need to see your solution (marriage coaching, in the above example), as only one of at least several possible solutions. In other words, don't get tied to your solution. If you do, you will put yourself in the position of having to defend it or prove it if it is challenged. Secondly, consider that there are always solutions and ways of doing things beyond what you can think of now.

Now that you are not tied to your solution, and have an open mind to other solutions, you can approach your spouse and honestly and positively present your goal (a better relationship), while omitting your solution (marriage coaching):

Example approach when using the method of agreement:
"I love you and I want my relationship with you to be even better than it is now."

Instead of negatively saying, "Our relationship has problems and we need to work on it," you positively say, "I love you and want our relationship to be even better." Although both of these statements has the same meaning, they provoke different reactions. They *feel* different—both to the person saying them and to the person hearing them. As you learn more about the agreement method, you will catch on, as my clients do, that loving messages work better than rejecting ones, no matter how "right" you are.

Please note that loving *and* being positive is different from simply being positive. It is positive to say, "I want our relationship to be much better," and that is ok to say if you already have a close relationship. In a strained relationship, it is too open to misinterpretation. The "I love you," loving message part, clarifies your motivation for wanting to work on the relationship.

Consider which <u>one</u> of these you would most like your spouse to say to YOU:
1. "Our relationship has problems and we need to work on them."

2. "I want our relationship to be much better."

3. "I love you and I want our relationship to be even better."

In a relationship, the way you say something is as important as what you say. After saying, "I love you and I want our relationship to be even better," you then wait for a response—any response at all. Don't get your hopes up that your partner will agree with you.

That would be too easy. Instead, you are wanting your partner to say *something*, good or bad, so that you can agree with him or her, as you will learn in the following sections.

If your partner agrees with you

If your partner does agree with you, then you can immediately start brainstorming together some ways to make your relationship better. (Brainstorming—coming up with multiple solutions—is an essential step in problem solving and will be covered in the chapter on problem solving).

Example conversation with an agreeable spouse:
YOU: *"I Love you and I want our relationship to be even better."*
SPOUSE: *"Me, too."*
YOU: *"Ok, let's make a list of some ways we could make our relationship better for both of us (brainstorming)."*

If your partner disagrees with you

If your partner disagrees with you, then you can agree with the disagreement. If she says, "I think our relationship is fine as it is. Any problems you have are in your mind." You can agree, that she is quite right, the problem is in your mind and on your mind, too. It's sometimes hard to think of anything else. Then she says, "Well you need to change the way you are thinking, not to be so psycho." You agree that would be great, you would love to think differently, although you are having a hard time with that. You ask her if she would brainstorm some ways to help you see how good the relationship is. And, again, you begin to cooperate.

Example conversation with a disagreeable spouse:
YOU: *"I Love you and I want our relationship to be even better."*
SPOUSE: *"I think our relationship is fine as it is. Any problems you have are in your mind."*

> *YOU: "You are right. I have some problems*
> *and they are on my mind a lot."*
> *SPOUSE: "Well, you need to change the way*
> *you are thinking—not to be so psycho."*
> *YOU: "That would be great. I would really*
> *like to. I have been having a hard time doing*
> *that. Would you help me to list some*
> *reasons why our relationship is so good?*
> *(brainstorming)"*

Agreeing with the disagreement brings you to the same place (cooperation) as if your spouse had agreed with you.

If your partner attacks you

If your spouse attacks you despite your loving message (but not with emotional or physical abuse), you would use agreement to calm him or her. Suppose your spouse says, "This relationship would already be much better if you weren't so damn selfish (you can substitute your spouse's favorite complaint about you here)." Remembering that it is agreement that will get you what you want rather than an argument, do you agree that you are selfish? No. "Selfish" is a name and don't participate in calling yourself names. It wouldn't sound sincere, anyhow.

Don't agree this way:
> *"You are right, I am selfish."*

Instead of agreeing that you are selfish, you can say, "I guess I do come across that way (can't be disputed since you are coming across that way to your spouse)." This may get followed by another attack, especially if your spouse is used to arguing with you. But, you would again use agreement (as you will learn more specifically in later chapters). Basically, you end up saying, "So, you would like me to be more helpful and giving in our relationship?" Your spouse should agree with you since you are agreeing with him or her. Remember, people don't fight against their own ideas. Then, you can say, "Ok, would you help me to think of some ways that would make it better for both of us?(brainstorming)" And, once again, you are off on problem solving, just as if your spouse had initially agreed with you.

Example discussion with an attacking spouse:
YOU: "I Love you and I want our relationship to be even better."
SPOUSE: "This relationship would already be much better if you weren't so damn selfish."
YOU: "I guess I do come across that way."
SPOUSE: "That's right, you never…."
YOU: "You are being really helpful in pointing these things out. Would you help me to think of some ways that would make our relationship better for both of us? (brainstorming)."

Part of using the method of agreement is deciding that it is more important to get to cooperation than it is to defend yourself. Defending yourself wouldn't change your spouse's mind—it would just make your spouse feel even more strongly about his or her opinions. Deciding to work on agreement is the fastest route to cooperation. Not only that, but you will be changing the way you and your spouse talk to each other to a more positive and productive one.

What if Your Spouse Won't Cooperate?

It would be natural for a spouse not to want to cooperate in something he or she disagreed with. But, in these examples, you are asking your spouse to cooperate in getting what he or she wants. Something that you agreed with. Any spouse who won't participate in working on getting what he or she wants to have anyway is very upset from a buildup of other issues. It's like offering meat to a dog with rabies. He will just ignore the meat and tear your arm off. So, if you want to say to me that this agreeing wouldn't work with such a person, then I agree with you. If you were my client, we would really need to concentrate on setting up some boundaries and work on earning respect before you even try to communicate this way to your spouse.

But, what I want you to consider here is that the other method, the debate/argument method, will provoke a fight even with very small differences. With such a rabid person, it would be just as useless as agreement but more explosive. Agreement might not work, but at least agreement won't make things worse. Agreement turns out to be a safe approach with everyone, although it won't work with everyone. It will, however, work much more often than any other method. Any gambler will tell you that if you have a method that will work more than half of the time, you can be rich. My advice is to play the odds and use agreement every time.

The agreement method helps people to get quickly to cooperation. Then, in the brainstorming work you can offer your idea as one of several possible ideas. Rather than defending your idea or attacking your partner's idea, you can discuss each idea together. If your idea really is the best, your spouse will convince herself or himself. If not, then you may convince yourself to try a different idea.

If you can understand this way of creating cooperation, then you can understand how people benefit from coaching. They learn skills that they use with their spouse to improve their relationship. Learning how to change the way you communicate can improve the relationship for both of you—even if your spouse is doing some seriously damaging things. For the remainder of this book, let me coach you to build your relationship, even if your spouse is the one who is making it difficult.

Agreement Improves Communication

If you have been using the debate method to try to resolve problems, you are going to love the agreement method. Typically with the debate method you have to go through a lengthy process of each of you trying to prove your point with breaks in between to recover emotionally. With the agreement method, there is no need for emotional recovery or repeated discussions about the same problem. You can put an end to conflict re-runs.

If you have a really serious problem, not everything will get resolved in one discussion, but one small part of the problem can get resolved each time. This means that you and your spouse will be continuously moving forward. The only time that you will get stuck with this method is if neither of you has any ideas for making your relationship better. That is no different from the limit of any other method you might use. If you reach such a point, then you will have an automatic "action" task of finding out what to do next. And, then you and your spouse can talk about ways to find out. Then, even though neither of you will have solutions, you will both be cooperating in finding some.

Moving forward and cooperating does wonders for communication. All differences can actually be opportunities to use the agreement process, which builds better communication, and results in sharing more and getting closer. The net result is that the differences in your relationship become opportunities for becoming closer rather than trials that push you apart. I believe that much of the excitement of differences is brought back by using this method. Spending my energy trying to turn my wife into another version of me is not my idea of a fun time. Sharing, and growing from our differences, is.

Couples who use the agreement method soon find that they can talk to their spouses more easily than they can to other people. This boosts their relationship in three ways: 1) it makes them more valuable for their spouses because they can talk about anything; 2) it helps them and their spouses to be more successful together than separately, since they are combining skills to solve problems and reach goals; and 3) it increases how secure each person feels because it becomes more obvious how important each partner is for each other. Agreement, done well, leads naturally to a Oneness Marriage.

Agreement Ends Power Struggles

Agreement is the great leveler. Because it leads to cooperation and input from both of you, each person's contribution is important. If you have ever felt belittled for your opinion, then you know what I am talking about when I say that disagreement, or debate, is the process of being on top by knocking the other person down. I don't want to play King on the Hill with my wife, especially because as I get older I think I am getting increasingly easier to knock off the hill.

Using agreement with a superior, such as your boss, will have the effect of lifting you up to his or her level. Using agreement with your kids will have the effect of lifting them up to your level (although you will still have the final say, just as your boss would). What this means is that the agreement method gives you more power without taking power away from others.

When you are good at using this method, you will not be able to be intimidated. In order for someone to intimidate you, they need to put you in a defensive position. If you have one of those know-it-all spouses who is super smart, this method is great for not letting them stupefy you with their intelligence. Intelligent people rely on their great reasoning power to outthink others. But when you are agreeing with them, their reasoning becomes useless!

Of course you could still be intimidated by abusive people. Again, that would be even more true with the debate method. In such situations emotional and physical safety come first. But, once that's in place, the agreement method can be used right away, whereas the debate method is much more likely to make the situation explosive again.

Greater Respect

You cannot make people respect you more by agreeing with everything they say. If that was what the agreement method was all about, then you would lose respect big time and your relationship would soon be over. But, since the agreement method uses a combination of *selective* agreement, good boundaries, and consistent messages of love, respect is built. When I see people working really hard on their relationships, but not making progress, it is usually either because their boundaries are too weak, their boundaries are too strong, or they have good boundaries but no message of love.

The debate method makes it really hard to say, "I love you." Can you imagine, "I love you, *but* I think you are wrong and let me tell you why"? That is certainly better than what most people say. But what tends to happen is that the "I love you," message gets canceled out by the disagreement, or filtered out by the other partner's defensiveness. With agreement, there is no cancelling out of the love message. "I love you, *and* I am concerned about that, too." Or, "I love you *and* I am glad you can tell me what's bothering you. You have a right to be upset." These messages, when they are delivered sincerely (all sarcasm is bad), *and* consistently, *and* followed up by cooperation, *and* good boundaries, make people's internal love meters go off the scale.

Are you married to someone who seems to love to argue? I call such people "Debaters." Debaters, typically suppress their debating before marriage because they know it is a turnoff, then resume debating once they are married. This makes debaters seem very different before and after they are married. The difference can be like night and day. After the debating begins, their partner's internal love meter can bottom out. It's simply hard to feel in love with a debater. If you are a man or woman who has a tendency to debate, you can get more love and commitment from people with less work. Instead of having to convince them to love you, you can create a natural desire in them to love you. Agreement is the real elixir of love.

Summary

With the debate method (method of argument), people selectively listen for what they disagree with and then ignore the rest of what was said. Each partner then goes for a personal win with logical arguments and examples. If their reasoning and examples should fail to convince, they emotionally attack each other. Even when this results in a "winner," it also results in an overall loss for the relationship. With debating, couples talk less and less, become more distant, lose respect for each other, and lose their loving feelings.

The agreement method takes the opposite approach from the debate method. With the agreement method, people selectively listen for what they agree with and ignore the rest. The goal is not to win, but to build cooperation. Although some differences will remain, the process of working together makes those differences easier to deal with. The relationship is restored to the way it was in the beginning, when people cared more about love than being right. As a result, couples enjoy talking more with each other, about more things, and become more emotionally intimate.

When the agreement method is combined with messages of love and good boundaries, it builds respect and security. The long term impact of the agreement method on a relationship is to increase how much each partner values the other. It also increases the depth of their love. The agreement method makes possible a Oneness Marriage—something that the debate/argument method cannot do.

♥2♥

WHY PEOPLE (LIKE YOU AND YOUR SPOUSE) DON'T AGREE

As you saw in the last chapter, there are many good reasons to agree and seemingly no downside. Although agreement won't always produce the results you want, neither will any of the other methods of working on problems. What this means is that agreement is your best first choice when there are important things to discuss, when your spouse is upset, or when you have a problem in your relationship. This chapter looks at some of the reasons why people are reluctant to agree and why you may be the only one you know who is using this method. It will also help you to understand why your partner doesn't agree with you, even when you are right.

Our Mental Autopilot

Security and survival are subconscious needs (below our level of awareness) that act as a filter for everything we do. If something is perceived at a subconscious level as a danger, we have an *automatic* resistance to it. What's more, any kind of change, good or bad, is recognized as a danger by our subconscious. That's why we often feel "butterflies" in our stomach when we are about to make a change, even if it is a good one. If someone else suggests we make a change, or tries to change us, our resistance is automatic and immediate. When we try to consciously change ourselves, we also encounter the same resistance. That's why changing is so hard.

Notice that we defend against or resist threats to our *way of life*. This is not the same as defending against threats to our *life*. We are used to doing things a certain way and we defend our unhealthy habits as well as our healthy ones. We struggle with change, even when we know what we are doing is not healthy and we consciously want to change. How easy life would be if we could simply select what habits we want to give up and which ones we want to add—"I'm going to think positively and never criticize my spouse again." As you know, it doesn't work that way.

Psychology has many ways for exploring the roots of your habits, which means basically how you learned them in the first place. Psychology has also made advances in understanding our *conscious* beliefs that maintain them. But, the 99% of the iceberg that is below the water—our subconscious—runs most of the show. And, our subconscious has a very basic survival mechanism. It works on the premise that whatever we did before and had some success with—no matter how small that success was—is the best thing to do again. You see, we don't really learn from our mistakes. We learn from our successes, even when they are partial. As far as the subconscious is concerned, a bird in the hand is better than a whole flock of birds in the bush.

I wrote my first book, *What to Do When He Won't Change* to help women to change their husband's destructive behaviors. In it I teach women that even if a man knows that his behavior is destructive to the relationship, as long as it works *a little* to get what he wants, he will have a very hard time stopping. That's why making him aware of problems does not automatically change his behavior. To help him to change, it is necessary to make sure that his behavior no longer benefits him at all. The same principle is also true for women.

First and foremost then, people don't use agreement because agreement is threatening to their own way of life. It is different from the way they usually communicate. Also, if you are different from me, and I agree with you, then that means that I might need to change. I won't stop to consider that changing might lead to self improvement and a better relationship. That's too rational and no matter how smart I am, I still react emotionally. I will tend to automatically defend my ideas, my thinking, my behavior, and my way of life—my lifestyle. I may even fight to the death (or at least to the destruction of my relationship) in order to defend my way of life, even if I am unhappy with it. If you don't believe that is true, all you have to do is to look at the destructive patterns that people continue to do. "I know I shouldn't, but...." Often people go right to the brink of the end of their relationship before they are willing to change. And then, it is often too late.

As you will see later, some people do change their habits and learn how to override their subconscious resistance. That is something you will need to do if you are to make the method of agreement work for you.

Why the First Years of Marriage Are Tough

The first couple of years of marriage bring to the surface all of the differences, both big and small, in how couples do things and how they think. Since our instinct is to defend our way of thinking, feeling, and behaving (they are all habits), it can be hard to tolerate differences in any area. There is a desire to "correct" the way our partners think, feel, and behave. If only they changed, we could feel more comfortable with them. Of course, our partners feel the same way.

Face it, if you try to get your partner to hang the toilet paper roll the opposite way from the way you do it, you are not doing that for your partner's sake. Your partner already feels fine with the way he or she hangs the toilet paper roll. I remember a heated argument that I had with a girlfriend when I was 22 years old. It was about the correct way to open a container of mustard. Talk about protecting a lifestyle! At that time, my relationship abilities were underdeveloped. I wish I could send a text message to myself back through time. I would say, "Jack, look at all she does for you.

Considering that, do you really care how she opens the mustard?" Unfortunately, I didn't learn that lesson during that relationship.

Fear of Rejection and Loss

Next to self-preservation, which we could also call "maintaining our identity," or "protecting our ego," the next strongest fear we encounter in relationships is the fear of rejection and abandonment. I always think this is one of the most ironic reasons that people argue and debate, since argument and debate make rejection and abandonment even more likely. People will fight so much over things that they believe are dangerous to their relationship that they destroy their relationship in the process.

To take an example of this, think about a husband who wants to go out with his friends but whose wife wants him to go out with her instead. In actuality, there is no right or wrong about either of these two options. Defensive reactions, however, immediately turn it into a right-wrong issue. Of course the husband is going to have reasons for wanting to go out with his friends and the wife is going to have reasons to want her husband to go out with her. They may each even use their relationship as a reason to defend their position.

The husband may say that he works all week for his family and needs some time for himself—that it helps him to de-stress and that his wife should be glad that he has a good way to do that.

The wife might argue that if they had a good time going out with each other, that would relieve the stress for *both* of them and make them closer at the same time. But, of course, that won't work for the husband because being with his wife *all the time* stresses him, even if they are going out doing something fun. But she will say that he *never* wants to spend time with her and that she doesn't know why he married her since he prefers to be with his friends *all the time*. Does that kind of arguing sound familiar to you?

The thing to notice in this example is that each person is focused on defending his or her own beliefs, feelings, and behaviors and there is *no* agreement about the needs of the other person. Another thing to notice is that the language becomes more extreme as the argument goes on. Words like "all the time" and "never" point to the underlying fears that each person has about the future, as they imagine the relationship continuing this way for the rest of their lives. They are not only fighting to protect their relationship now, they are fighting to protect the worst thing they can imagine happening in the future. He is afraid that he won't be able to see his friends again and will be a prisoner in his own home. She is afraid that he will abandon her for his friends.

You can see that at this point, if one of them gives in, that the other partner will still not be happy about it. And the one who gives in will be resentful. In their own way, each of them is trying to keep the relationship an enjoyable one for both the present and the future. But their way of going about making that happen worsens the problem. It increases the emotional distance between them.

Fears of abandonment—what I often call *neediness*—become destructive when we try to make our partner relieve our fears by reassurance or sacrifice. When we sacrifice voluntarily for our partners, that is part of love. When we ask our partners to sacrifice for us because we feel insecure, it damages the relationship.

The beliefs of a needy and insecure partner:
"I don't trust you to be able to maintain a loving relationship with me, so I need to continually test the status of our relationship and be sure you are doing what I want. Anything you do that is different from what I think, feel, do, or desire, is a rejection of the way that I am. So, I need to eliminate or avoid all differences and repeatedly check in with you to make sure everything is alright."

Can you imagine the wife or husband in the above example (about going out with friends or as a couple) thinking about agreeing with her or his spouse? In their minds, agreement would mean sacrifice and a weakening of the relationship. Insecurity and obligation are not words that fit well with a close relationship.

As you will see in later chapters, there is a big difference between agreement and giving-in. Giving in is a concession, which done repeatedly leads to resentment and loss of loving feelings. Agreement leads to connection and cooperation, which result in a closer relationship.

Fear of Being Powerless

Everyone wants to feel like they have the personal power to control their destiny. This doesn't mean that they want to use their power to dominate others. I would tend to call that "aggressiveness" or "domination" rather than "power." Power is a good thing. You can see it in young children when they create a drawing with their crayons, get a good grade at school, or score a goal. Personal power gives people feelings of effectiveness which are captured in expressions like "I did it!" and "I can do it!"

How is this connected with not agreeing with people? Consider this chain of thinking:

> *"If I agree with you, I am doing things your way. You are not doing things my way.*
> *And, if I am always agreeing with you, then I will always be doing things your way. Which means this relationship will be the way that you want it. And I will have to go along with you, like a rudderless boat carried on a huge wave. Who I am will be lost at sea."*

This kind of thinking goes on very fast at a subconscious level. Debating or arguing is thus a way to defend against feeling powerless or against losing our self identity.

It is another ironic situation, since debating and arguing actually lead to a loss of control over the relationship, which becomes increasingly distant the more we try to get our own way. Ultimately, our partners may leave us, making us not only feel powerless, but unlovable as well. Rejection doesn't do anything good for our self identity.

The correct use of loving communication gives us the power to keep our relationships strong and our partners attracted to us. Politicians know this very well. Agreement is power. They agree with whomever they are talking to, which results in making other people feel good about themselves and the politician. You can't make people feel better about you by making them feel worse about themselves. Can you imagine what would happen if politicians disagreed with the people they talk to? If thinking about politicians turns you off, consider how people talk when they are first dating. They emphasize similarities and agreement so that their dates will continue to want to go out with them.

Communication Style Is a Habit

The number one reason that people don't use agreement to handle differences is that it is not their habit to do so. Habits come naturally and easily and so always feel like the right thing to do at the moment. Only hindsight shows our habits to be harmful. People who argue and debate feel it is the right thing to do at the moment they are doing it. "She said something that was really stupid and wrong, so I just had to correct her." Oh really? Why is that?

Habits are maintained by partial success. If a woman nags her husband, she may not get compliance most of the time. But, if it works one time in ten, she will continue to do it—even if it is damaging her relationship. It is only if her relationship is put in danger that she will think twice about nagging. And, she may not stop nagging until after she has actually lost her relationship. The partial-reward-maintains-behavior principle is wonderfully illustrated by casino slot machines. People will put in quarter after quarter (or token after token), as long as they sometimes receive a payout—even if overall they lose money. If you put an "out of order" sign on the slot machine, however, no one will play it. When there is zero payoff, people change.

I regularly teach my coaching clients how to use agreement to rebuild their relationship. They are ready to learn because their relationship is severely threatened. Until they get to that point, habit dominates. Only a small percentage of people try to get more by looking for new ways to do things. The typical strategy is to try even harder to do what they are already doing. If arguing helps one time out of ten, then when they feel their relationship is threatened, they will argue more to try to have success again. No one would argue if they thought they couldn't win.

It is essential to understand this process when you are changing to an agreement style of communication. Whenever you change the way you communicate with your partner, your partner will escalate his or her typical behaviors (make more effort) to try to have success and to return things to "normal." Your partner has to experience his or her habit no longer working for some time before he or she will begin to change. The process is like this: 1) you change your communication style; 2) he or she tries really hard to maintain the same way of communicating and finally gives up, 3) then, the communication improves for both of you. This means that when you are working on positive changes, your partner behaving worse than usual is a sign that you are making progress. People who don't understand this give up when their partner's behavior gets worse and conclude that the new way is no good. Make sure that doesn't happen to you.

Another example illustrating this is that of parents learning to help their child overcome temper tantrums. If the parents decide they are going to deal with this by ignoring their child's tantrums, then at first their child's tantrums will get louder and longer. This is because their child will be trying extra hard to make his or her way (having a tantrum) work again. If the parents are consistent and persistent, the tantrum behavior will start to drop off after this period of increased tantrums. But, if they give in just one time in 10, they will have taught their child to tantrum longer and louder. Their giving in will ensure that the tantrum behavior will continue for a very long time.

We change other people's habits by making them not work with us anymore. At all. Zero.

Agreement and Personal Distance

You probably already know that everyone has a physical comfort zone. It's the physical distance that they maintain between themselves and other people. If they are comfortable standing one meter from you and you stand less than a meter from them, they will back up. If you stand more than a meter away, they will come closer. When two people with different comfort zones meet, the one who doesn't like being so close may change the angle of his or her body, avoid eye contact, cross his or her arms, or hold an object between the two of them. Although physically close, such behavior helps make the distance feel more comfortable.

People also have an emotional comfort zone. And when you are getting too close emotionally, they will use disagreement, debate, criticism, or refusal, to create a "safe" distance again. It is an emotional way for them to cross their arms.

Agreement has the potential to draw people emotionally much closer. While one partner may desire this, the other partner may not. Seemingly meaningless arguments (e.g., how to open a mustard container) often have this purpose of pushing someone back to a comfortable distance from us. It's also not uncommon to alternate between needing space and wanting to be closer.

Did you ever have one grandparent who was lovey dovey while the other was cranky? Perhaps grandpa was trying to keep you at a comfortable distance while grandma was trying to bring you in closer. An emotional comfort zone really explains a lot of human behavior and you may be able to get good insight into the behavior of your family members just from considering this. The more someone has been emotionally hurt, the more emotional distance they will tend to create.

Even more important than observing others is to observe yourself to see if you keep people at emotional arm's length by use of sarcasm and disagreement. Has someone close to you hurt you before? If so, you may have learned that a safe emotional distance is not a close one.

Fortunately, even people who have a very tough time trusting others can learn to overcome their fears and improve their relationships.

People Don't Know How to Agree

This has to be the number two reason that people don't agree (number one is habit). Disagreement seems to be learned at a very young age. To disagree, we pick out parts of what someone is saying that we don't agree with and then express that without mentioning anything that we agree with. It is a skill of selective listening.

People tend to be naturally poor at using selective listening for agreement. When people try to use agreement, they often just make a blanket statement such as, "I agree with you." There is no attempt to listen and pick out parts of what someone is saying and agree with just those parts. This blanket agreement is not very effective when people have conflict. It is often insincere and manipulative, it feels like giving in, and it leads to resentment.

The correct use of agreement is very similar to that for disagreement. That is, agreement involves selective listening, and not blanket agreement. It means focusing on what you agree with while putting any disagreements aside. Although it sounds easy, it takes considerable practice to do well. Disagreement is fast and natural in the American culture. If someone says to me, "I like the Red Sox," it would be more natural for me to say, "I prefer the Yankees," or "Their ok, but I like the Yankees better." It is not natural for most Americans to leave their disagreement out and say "The Red Sox have some really strong players," without voicing their disagreement.

Or, to use a relationship example, if my wife tells me she would like to go shoe shopping (her favorite sport), it is easier for me to say "I hate shoe shopping," than to say, "You are really good at choosing fashionable shoes (which she is)." As long as our relationship is strong, this won't be a big deal. But, in a weak relationship, too many of these disagreements can create a distance that is hard to recover from.

Some People Don't Want to Be Your Friend

This reason is similar to people wanting to maintain their distance, but the difference is that when you pull away, they don't move closer. That is, they are not trying to keep the *same* distance from you, but rather they are moving out of relationship with you or *preventing* a relationship with you.

It is easy to imagine a secretary intentionally not being agreeable with a boss who is getting too personal or coming on to her. But, it also happens in marriages. There comes a time in a bad relationship when people become motivated to leave it. At that point, even if you are agreeing with them, they won't want to agree with you.

People are emotional beings. They can't just rationally decide to leave their partner due to incompatibility. They have to *feel* that they are incompatible, too. One way to do that is to intentionally be argumentative. You might buy your spouse a chocolate cake because you know that she loves it, but after you buy it she says, "Why did you buy that? I hate chocolate cake." You will probably say, "I thought it was your favorite," to which she might reply, "Well, not anymore, get it out of here—I don't want to have to look at it." You say, "Well, what do you want me to do with it, throw it away?" to which she says, "I don't care what you do with it." If she lets it go at that you will be lucky. The fact is that even if she knows how to agree and knows it would be good for your relationship, she no longer wants the relationship. She doesn't want you to be nice while she is preparing (mentally if not physically) to leave you. Remember, people mentally check out of a relationship before they physically check out of it.

Should you argue with people when they are like that? Not unless you want to speed up the demise of your relationship with them. A person who no longer wants a relationship with you is a person who has lost respect for you. Reconnecting with them is

27

going to involve the use of agreement, but also the use of boundaries to build respect. Agreement connects, but only boundaries create respect. The following chapters will teach you how to use agreement and boundaries together to improve your relationship.

Summary

The reasons why people don't use agreement come down to three things: 1) habit, 2) lack of communication skills, and 3) insecurities. The insecurities are either about giving up one's personal identity, becoming less powerful, or becoming too emotionally close for comfort. If you find yourself having a hard time using agreement, you will need to figure out which of these three reasons is your main obstacle, and then deal with it.

♥3♥

PROBLEM SOLVING WITH YOUR PARTNER
MADE EASY

The method of agreement takes you all the way—right up to the door of solving conflict, in a way that disagreement and debate can never do. Disagreement and debate lead to each person becoming more strongly convinced of his or her opinion. The only ways to resolve such a polarized difference are to: 1) give-in, 2) compromise, or 3) agree to disagree. None of these are win-win. The more these three ways are used, the more relationships fall apart. Win-win can only be accomplished with the method of agreement and problem solving.

The main reason that disagreement cannot lead to problem solving is that there is no common definition of the problem. Without a common definition, there can be no cooperation. Take for example the following exchange:

> *PARTNER1: "If you weren't so stubborn we could get along better."*
> *PARTNER2: "If you weren't so unreasonable, I wouldn't have to be so stubborn."*

The problem definitions are different. One person believes the problem to lie in the other person's stubbornness, and the other person believes the problem to lie in the partner's unreasonableness. If one of them attempts to do problem solving at this point, it will lead to more conflict:

> **PARTNER2: "Let's work on some ways that you can be more reasonable, so I don't have to be so stubborn."**
> **PARTNER1: "I am reasonable. You're the one with the problem."**

And off the couple will go again in their debate, probably getting more emotional, too.

People have to first agree on what a problem is before they will be willing to work on it together. The method of agreement brings people to that point naturally, as in the following example:

> **PARTNER1: "You never listen to me."**
> **PARTNER2: "Yes, I'm probably not doing a very good job listening to you, or at least I'm not making you feel listened to."**
> **PARTNER1: "That's right."**
> **PARTNER2: "Ok, let's work on coming up with some ways that could help you to feel like I am listening well."**
> **PARTNER1: "Ok."**

During the problem solving that follows, the couple will talk positively about how to make things better for both of them and come up with one or two win-win solutions. I have walked hundreds of couples and thousands of individuals through this process in relationship counseling and coaching. It works every time and couples like it. In this chapter, I will teach you how to do this with your partner, your child, your parent, your boss, your friend, or whomever you would ordinarily have major disagreements with.

Problem Solving Overview

There are many different methods of problem solving. The method that I am going to teach you can be used for almost all situations. There are five steps to this method:

1. Positively agreeing on the problem
2. Brainstorming solutions
3. Comparing solutions
4. Choosing a solution
5. Choosing a backup solution

Step One: Positively Agreeing on the Problem

You saw an example of this above. It is a natural product of using the agreement method. This is the step that makes people *want to* work together cooperatively. To be effective, it needs to be stated in positive terms.

Let's compare positive and negative problem statements:

Negative problem statement:
We both fight a lot and don't listen to each other.
Positive problem statement:
We want to get along better and listen to each other more.

The negative statement would lead to reasons for the fights. And where is that most likely to lead?...to more fighting! The positive statement leads to ideas about making things better.

Let's consider another example:

Negative problem statement:
"We spend too much money on luxuries."
Positive problem statement:
"We need to be able to pay our bills."

31

The negative statement does lead to a possible solution, but only to one—spending less money on luxuries. As with most simple solutions, it's easier said than done and is less likely to work. The second, positive problem statement, leads to multiple solutions such as making a budget, working overtime, reducing expenses, and getting advice from a financial consultant.

Don't be in such a hurry to get to solutions that you skip this step

Before you even think about getting to solutions, write down what you both agree on. Make any necessary changes to make sure you both really agree. This method won't work if people only pretend to agree. Pretending to agree is not agreement—it is lying, deception, manipulation, or even worse—sarcasm. Don't be in such a hurry to find solutions that you don't get to a common definition of the problem. That would be like being in such a hurry to go on a road trip that you didn't bother to put gas in the car. Without a common definition, you won't get very far.

Be sure you write it down

There are multiple reasons for this. The first is that problem solving is too complex a process to do in your head. Even if you are a genius, you will not be able to do problem solving well in your head. Another reason to write it down is to make sure that you and your partner are actually agreeing on the same problem definition. People hear what they want to hear and people miss what they want to miss. Writing down the problem statement and asking your partner to agree or change it so that he or she does agree is part of productive communication. If this process is new to you, just coming to such an agreement will be a big improvement.

After you have written it down and both agreed, change it into a positive form if it isn't already. So, "We fight too much" becomes "How to get along." "We overspend" becomes "How to save money." "John doesn't feel listened to," becomes "How to help John feel listened to," "Going out is no fun," becomes "How to have more fun when we go out," and so on. Then, once again make sure you are both in agreement about this positively worded problem definition.

If you are doing this with a young child, you and your child can draw a picture. An example of a negative picture would be a monster hiding under the bed. This could be redrawn to a positive picture of your child feeling happy at bedtime. "Ok, Sarah, we don't want this one, right? (show picture of monster under bed), we want this one, right? (show picture of happy Sarah at bedtime)." Drawings also work with adults and can add a touch of humor to the situation.

Step Two: Brainstorming Solutions

This step is the fun part. I mean that literally. It is in this step that people can be creative and come up with any ideas, no matter how wild or crazy they may seem. "Brainstorming" is letting ideas come out of your head without any kind of censorship or evaluation. The idea is that when you do this, you unblock creative solutions that are usually below your level of awareness.

Each partner needs to come up with some solutions and all of the solutions need to be written down. *None* of the solutions are discussed in this step. Let's consider a hypothetical example.

Example: Brainstorming solutions to the common problem definition of "how to save money."
Idea one: Sell the children
Idea two: Start our own business
Idea three: Make a budget
Idea four: Live on beans and rice
Idea five: Rob a bank
Idea six: Sell the junk in the attic
Idea seven: ?

In this example, the couple got stuck after coming up with six ideas. Since five ideas are enough, they have completed this step. If you are bothered by the "sell the children" idea, you should know that I have heard this and similar ideas many times in doing this exercise with couples. Children are a major expense and it is natural that this idea would come up. Would anyone actually do this? Of course not, but being able to let the idea come out opens up the way for other ideas. Also, many of my clients have fun hearing the ideas that come out.

This step is simply listing ideas until there are at least five. There should be NO DISCUSSION or elaboration of these ideas in this step. That would only get in the way of creative problem solving. The more ideas you can come up with, the better. Sometimes, the first nine ideas a person comes up with will be pretty lousy and then the tenth will be right on.

Step Three: Comparing Solutions

In this step, you and your partner will talk about the pros and cons (otherwise known as costs and benefits) of each solution. What you need to realize is that *every* idea, no matter how crazy it may seem on the surface, has both costs and benefits. You can list these after the ideas, drawing a minus "-"next to the costs (cons) and a plus "+" next to the benefits (pros). So, for the above example, it might look like this:

Idea one: Sell the children
+would reduce all our expenses
+we could get a smaller home
+wouldn't need to worry about college
-it would be hard to find a buyer
-we would miss them
-our parents would be upset
-we might have to go to prison

Idea two: Start our own business
-there are start up costs for business
-might not be successful
+could do what we really wanted to do

> *+wouldn't have to be tied to living where we*
> *are*
> *-would have to learn how to run a business*
> *+could start small, just part time*

Each of the other ideas would be considered in the same way. Couples may spend more than an hour on this step. There are a lot of things to talk about, and the talking is very pleasant compared to previous disagreements. In the process of talking about these ideas, you and your partner may come up with additional ideas that can be added to the list.

There is no reason that this step (or all the steps) can't be accomplished at your favorite coffee shop or pub. It is a social event. It is you and your partner talking in a positive way about something that concerns you both and has the potential to make your life and relationship much better. Again and again couples tell me this was the best thing they did in their coaching.

Step Four: Choosing a Solution

Now that you have compared all of the different solutions, you will be in good shape for choosing one. What you will have discovered in comparing the pros and cons is that there is no perfect solution—there never is. You also may be quite surprised to find that the best solution is not one either of you had originally considered. It's part of what makes problem solving fun.

When you choose a solution, you need to consider it to be an *experiment*. There may be costs associated with it that neither of you considered, or something else may make it difficult or impractical. Just knowing that you are not going to be locked into a solution, if it is not working, should make it easier to choose one. Too often, people become locked into the idea that there is only one solution and if that doesn't work, the jig is up—time to end the relationship. That couldn't be further from the truth! There are always other possibilities. What makes me excel at my job is simply that I know more solutions and methods than the average person does. Coming to a road block doesn't mean that there is no more road. It just means that it is time to find some other way to keep moving ahead.

Choosing your solution on paper is as simple as drawing a circle around it. The solution you choose is not really related to the number of plus signs or minus signs you have under it. Because these are subjective evaluations, you can't compare them mathematically. Having talked through them will help you and your partner to have a *feel* for what is the best solution. Another couple, with the same ideas, might agree on a totally different solution.

Step Five: Choosing a Backup Solution

This step is very important. Having a backup solution will take some of the pressure off having to have the first solution work. You and your partner won't need to have an internal, "Oh no, what if this doesn't work?" Your first choice is simply an experiment—it will be great if it works, but if it doesn't then there are other things to try. Many men have been drawn into couples coaching this way. Their wives work with them to come up with solutions to a difficult marriage problem and they decide on a solution. But, they also have a backup solution, such as getting marriage coaching if their first idea doesn't work out. People are much more willing to try your idea if you will try their idea first.

At the time you agree to their idea, you get them to agree with your backup plan, like this:

> *YOU: "Ok, let's try your idea for a month.*
> *But, if it's not working, will you try my*
> *idea?"*
> *PARTNER: "Ok, if you really try my way."*
> *YOU: "I will."*

One reason people are more willing to try your idea when theirs doesn't work is that they usually don't have their own backup plan. After people think of one solution, they don't try to think of other solutions. That is a weakness that the problem solving approach avoids. There is no single "best" solution, but there is one that is more likely to work. And, if that one doesn't, then you have another one you can try next.

Draw a circle around your second choice and also write "#2" next to it. When you have done that, you have finished problem solving this particular issue. It's quite possible to do in one hour what you and your spouse have not been able to do in months or even years of arguing. And, unlike arguing, this process is collaborative, which means it will draw you together.

Troubleshooting

"What if we can't agree on the problem?"

Then, you need to practice the agreement method some more. It's not necessary to agree on the most central issue. If you both agree on some small part of the problem, it's enough to begin working on it. For example, if your partner thinks your relationship is doomed, but you want to get marriage coaching, then you are both at polar opposites. But, you both may agree that no matter what happens to your marriage, it will be good if you can communicate better. Taking this "piece" of the problem to work on can actually improve your marriage. The reason for that is that collaboration brings increased closeness no matter what you are working on.

"What if we start to argue when we are problem solving?"

If you argue when problem solving, it is most likely because you have gotten off track. One thing to try if that happens is to agree with your partner to work on that issue (which you are arguing about) at another time, but say that you can only work on one issue at a time. If your partner is unwilling to do that, then postpone the problem solving. It won't work with argument. Keep working on using the agreement method. You will get another chance to do problem solving soon. Don't be upset if your partner doesn't finish the problem solving with you. If he or she started it with you, then be appreciative of how he or she went a step further than usual. Improving a relationship is a marathon, not a pole vaulting event.

"What if we can't think of five solutions?"

Then, don't go on to the next step. Five is a minimum number. Remember, you don't have to have great solutions during the brainstorming step—any will do. If you can't think of a serious one, think of a silly one. Don't be afraid to put in bad solutions. They can be very helpful during the discussion. For example, if one of the solutions is "We can divorce," although neither of you wants to do that, discussing the pros and cons can help your partner be more committed to the relationship. He or she may not have considered the downside to divorce in any detail.

Discussing the pros and cons of ideas gives a structure to your talking that you would not have been able to have just in a typical discussion. Knowing that all ideas are both good and bad will help you to discuss both aspects. It takes away the need for either of you to be strongly attached to an idea, to defend your idea, or to attack the other person's idea.

"How long should we try a solution before going to a backup solution?"

This is not an exact science. If the main solution is obviously not going to work, then you can both agree to abandon it. But, as long as one of you still thinks it's a good idea, it is best to stick with it for a month. By then, you should have some indication of whether it is going to work.

"What if the backup solution doesn't work either?"

At the time you move to using your backup solution, you should choose a new backup solution. This way, you always have two possible solutions to try.

"What if none of our solutions work?"

It is a good idea to have a default solution of going to marriage counseling or getting marriage coaching, if they are not already included in your list of solutions. One advantage of this being your default solution is that you and your partner will be more willing to work in counseling or coaching if all other ideas have failed.

Although my clients have already tried to do what they know how to do to improve their relationship, usually that amounts to only a couple of things. There are many different approaches to improving a relationship and many different skills that can help. To prove my point I offer a money back guarantee to my clients if I can't help them find loving ways to improve their relationship. Although I have been counseling and coaching since 1994, I have yet to have a client where there was not something more we could do.

For every relationship problem that exists, at least some other people have been able to overcome it without divorcing. That means that there are still other solutions to try. If only five out of 100 people with your problem are able to resolve it, that doesn't mean you should give up. It means you should find out what those five people are doing and do that yourself.

Summary

The purpose of debate/argument is to win one's point. It can only lead to giving in, compromise, or continued disagreement. These three outcomes damage relationships, especially when they are done often. On the other hand, the agreement method paves the way for a true win-win solution.

The agreement method creates a desire to work together. When the agreement method is followed by problem solving, couples are no longer stuck, but can work together on positive solutions. Problem solving is done on paper. It is a structured, positive way, to hear each other out and to arrive at a mutually satisfying solution, as well as a backup plan. With problem solving, solutions are considered to be experiments which can be discarded if they don't work. This helps couples to cooperate in implementing their solutions.

Selfishness is not living as one wishes to live, it is asking others to live as one wishes to live.

Oscar Wilde
Irish Dramatist, Novelist, & Poet

♥4♥

USING AGREEMENT WITH EVERYDAY
SITUATIONS AND SELFISHNESS

This chapter will start you off using the method of agreement in your everyday conversation. As is my way, I will teach you how to use agreement with difficult situations. If you can do that, you won't need any help using agreement in easy situations. In particular, I will teach you how to use agreement when your spouse, significant other, or friend is being selfish.

Recognizing Selfishness

There are many ways to be selfish and I will give you examples of how to use the method of agreement with several different kinds. In truth, we can say that anything that your partner is doing which harms your relationship is selfish. So, of course affairs are selfish, emotional abuse is selfish, one sided sexual satisfaction is selfish, etc. This chapter will not go into these subjects in depth. These are such big issues I have devoted entire chapters to them later on.

Selfishness is a matter of type and degree. An affair is an extreme of selfishness from the first instance. But, other kinds of selfishness build up gradually. If you had spent time preparing a romantic dinner, for example, and your partner goes out for dinner with a coworker, that may or may not be selfish. But, the more it happens, the more you can be sure that it is selfish. And, the more it happens, the more selfish it becomes.

There are still lesser degrees of selfishness. For example, when your partner starts to desire to watch TV or surf the internet rather than to go to bed with you. When it happens once in a while, it's probably just sleeplessness, but if it happens more and more, it amounts to selfishness. And then there is the kiss goodbye that turns into a wave goodbye, which turns into nothing but the sound of the door clicking shut and the car starting.

An affair that happens just one time is enough to deal a severe blow to a marriage, but the impact of these daily smaller selfish actions can have an *even bigger* impact. It's these daily, smaller things that I will address in this chapter. The sooner you catch them and the sooner you communicate (not complain) to your partner about them, the better off you both will be. If you were to depend on the debate method instead of the method of agreement, you would postpone talking about these problems as long as you could, which would just allow more damage to be done to your relationship.

The Debate Method and Selfishness

We can learn more about agreeing if we take a look at the contrasting use of agreement and debate. Many people question their spouse when they see a behavior they don't like with questions such as, "John, why do you need to use the computer until 2:00 am every night?" In a troubled relationship, such questions are perceived as attacks. They are likely to bring counter questions like, "What's wrong with surfing the internet?" You also may get a finger pointed back at you. "You have a lot more free time than I do. Nighttime is about the only time I can have a little peace and quiet by myself."

People also pose nonverbal questions with their behavior. For example, they may put extra passion into their kiss goodbye and see how their spouse responds. If they don't get a passionate response it's a kind of nonverbal reply. If they then verbally ask about it, they may get a verbal reply such as, "Do you think couples always have to be passionate when they kiss goodbye?" These kinds of responses from your spouse are designed to get you to drop the subject. And, that's probably what you would do with the method of debate—at least for now.

As time goes on though, your spouse's behavior would stay the same or worsen. You might get used to having more distance in your relationship, although it would still bother you at a deeper level. You would start to feel a loss of emotional connection. You would envision the distance between you growing as you think about the future. You might think, "Will we still be together five years from now? Will there be any feelings left at all?" If you are like most people, at first you would shake it off and tell yourself that you are exaggerating. You would attempt again to be closer to your spouse, probably with the same poor results. You would be sensing that something needs to change. And of course, you would be right. Then your thoughts and words might start coming out as "wishes." "I wish we could go out together more often," "I wish you would spend more time with the kids," I wish you would sleep with me at night," and so on. How much you actually say will probably depend on how bad of a reaction you imagine your spouse will have.

Although you would only be expressing your desire to be together, your spouse is likely to become defensive and to hear, "I wish you were different/a better partner/a better parent/more like me so I would be happier." Your spouse will react to your wishes as though he or she were being blamed. Depending on your spouse's habits, he or she will either defend—"I take you out lots of times…;" counterattack—"All you think about is yourself, it's no picnic going to work every day/taking care of the kids every day/putting up with your mother all the time;" actively avoid by not responding; or passively avoid by making promises without following through on them.

And, so the distance in your relationship would escalate. Notice that the escalations would take place precisely at the times that you communicate about your desires. Every time you talk about things, they get worse. It's as if the communication about the problems is what pushes the relationship even further apart.

Because poor communication adds to problems, couples usually stop communicating when the pain level gets too much to bear and when the communication is obviously making things worse. We could take these examples on to further stages of more intense conflict, or to the point where you or your spouse gives up on trying to change things. At that point, you will have a lonely, distant relationship which is even more likely to end.

As you see, small problems can, and often do, build into big ones. What determines whether they do is not *what* the particular problems are, but the *way you communicate* about them. The question and debate method of communication results in increasing distance and worsening problems. Every verbal or physical rejection and argument becomes like another straw on the camel's back—threatening to crush your love and your relationship under the weight.

Fortunately, there is a better way of communicating that will prevent differences from growing into problems—a way to communicate that makes things better rather than worse. It's time to get to it.

Making a Clear Request

The first step should always be a clear communication about what you want rather than a question about something you don't want. This initial communication isn't agreement per se, because so far you have nothing to agree with. Clear requests are often so effective that no further methods are needed. Here are examples of fuzzy and clear communication about wanting your spouse to go to bed with you rather than staying up watching TV or using the computer:

Fuzzy communication:
> *"John, I wish we could sleep together like we used to."*

This is fuzzy because John would have to guess what you really mean. Does "wishing" it mean that you realize that you can't, and that's too bad? Does "like we used to" mean having sex every night like when you were first married? Does it mean you sleep on the left side of the bed and he sleeps on the right? And so on. In my coaching work, I hear fuzzy communication happening in almost every relationship.

Clear communication:
"John, I want you to go to bed at the same time as me every night."

This communication is clear and it is neither a demand, nor a complaint. What seems to surprise my clients the most is that often their partner will simply agree with them and do what they want. Here are some more examples of fuzzy and clear communication.

Fuzzy:
"I wish you would do something with your dirty clothes."
Clear:
"I want you to put your dirty clothes in the hamper every time you take them off."

Fuzzy:
"I wish you would be more careful about how you use the credit cards."
Clear:
"I want us to make a budget and to set a limit on how much we can charge on the credit cards."

The idea is that if you communicate clearly, the other person will have a fair chance of being able to give you what you want. If you are thinking, "I shouldn't have to say what I want," then likely you are out of touch with reality. If your partner is not doing something, then you *do* have to say. If you don't like to say, then it is something for you to work on. Until your partner refuses with words or behavior, you have little to complain about. Always make a clear request before moving on to other methods.

Next, we will consider what to do when your spouse does not respond well to your clear requests.

Using Agreement to End Financial Selfishness

There is a separate chapter for dealing with major financial problems using the method of agreement. Here, let's consider some common minor ones. Imagine your partner is spending a lot of money on his or her entertainment, while you only have a little to spend. You are careful not to spend too much because you know that paying the bills is important. Your partner doesn't have any problem spending money because he or she can see that the bills are being paid. This is one of these situations where your resentment will increase over time if you don't do something.

The first step, as noted in the previous section, would be to make a clear request, such as:

Your clear request:
"Each pay period, I would like us to set aside the money we need to pay the bills and to save for our retirement. Then, we can divide the remaining money equally to use as our own spending money."

Now, we will suppose that your partner disagrees and see how you can respond to that. There are many possible ways your partner could respond, but considering three will help you to understand how to handle other responses.

Example: Using agreement with an inconsiderate response
YOUR PARTNER: "I think things are fine as they are."

YOU: "Yes, we are able to pay our bills, with the way we are doing things now."

YOUR PARTNER: "Ok then, we don't need to change anything."

YOU: "Yes, we could just keep things as they are and you are right that it would work in the short term."

YOUR PARTNER: "What do you mean?"

YOU: "Well, the most important thing for me is our relationship. So, I think it's important that we both feel good about the way we use our money."

YOUR PARTNER: "Well, I feel fine about it."

YOU: "Yes, and I am glad you do and I want you to be able to enjoy yourself."

YOUR PARTNER: "Then, what's your problem?"

YOU: "You are right, I have a problem. There are things I want to do, too, but I don't know how we can afford it."

YOUR PARTNER: "Like what?"

YOU: "Well, would you help me do a little problem solving about it, so that we can both feel good about the way we use the money?"

YOUR PARTNER: "I guess so..."

At this point, you would start the problem solving (see problem solving chapter). You can do this because you have not put your partner on the defensive and have actually made supportive statements. If you were to use the debate method, instead of getting to problem solving you would end up arguing about fairness and selfishness. It would lead to greater distance rather than resolving the problem.

If your partner refused to problem solve, then you would need to use some boundaries such as looking for a job and telling your partner that you will be unable to cook/clean/do childcare, etc. in order to make time for your job. With the boundaries in place, your partner will be more likely to do problem solving with you. Note that boundaries are a decision *you* make and an action *you* take—there is no debate about it.

Example: Using agreement with a controlling response

PARTNER: "I make the money, I will decide how to use it. If you want more money, then you can get a job."

YOU: "Yes, you do make the money and I am very proud of you for supporting us. I agree that getting a job would be a way for me to have more money, too. Would you sit down with me and help me figure out what kind of job to get and the changes we would need to make in our lifestyle?"

PARTNER: "What do you mean, changes?"

YOU: "Well, it takes time to make money, and energy too. So, I probably won't be able to help out as much around the house and depending on my schedule, it could interfere with some of the things we do together."

PARTNER: "Well, I don't see why you need more money. I give you enough."

YOU: "Yes, it would be difficult for many people to see. If you would like to go over it together, I would be happy to do that."

PARTNER: "How much do you need?"

YOU: "Half of the extra money, after we pay the bills and contribute to our savings."

PARTNER: "Well, that's not going to happen."
YOU: "Ok, thank you for telling me clearly. I won't ask you about it again."
PARTNER: "So, what are you going to do?"
YOU: "Well, if you help me, then we can figure out some things together. If not, then I will figure them out on my own."

In this example, you can clearly see the boundary element. There is no attempt to force your partner to either comply with your wishes or to work with you. Trying to control a controller just leads to explosions. Instead, there is the consistent message that you are not going to argue, and neither are you just going to give up. You will make the changes necessary to make your relationship more fair, with or without your partner's help.

Consistently communicating like this (i.e. positive, agreeable, inviting, and with good boundaries) will gradually change the way your partner communicates with you. This is because he or she needs to feel powerful, but will only have a chance to do so by doing the problem solving work with you. It's the only way for him or her not to be left out of the decisions, which is very hard to tolerate for a controlling person.

Example: Using agreement with a blaming response

PARTNER: "You are always money hungry. I provide everything you need and you still want more."
YOU: "Yes, you are a very good provider. Thank you."
PARTNER: "But, you're not satisfied."
YOU: "Maybe a lot of people would think that I should be, but you're right—I'm not satisfied."
PARTNER: "You are never satisfied."

> **YOU: "I guess many times I'm not, you're right."**

Here you can see the deliberate attempt by your partner to draw you into a fight, make you feel guilty, and relieve him or her of responsibility. In this example, you don't get defensive, but admit that from his perspective he is right. Keep in mind that your purpose is not to win an argument, not to defend yourself, and not to be right. Focusing on making your partner right will be more helpful in getting to cooperation.

Example: Handling a verbally abusive response (no agreement)

> **PARTNER: "You are a money hungry bitch."**
> **YOU: (Immediately leave).**

I put in an extra disagreement here just in case you have a verbally abusive spouse. In this example, you can see your partner resort to verbal abuse by calling you a bad name. Never use the method of agreement with verbal abuse. You will lose respect and the verbal abuse will be even worse in the future. Eliminating verbal abuse requires an immediate boundary action from the *first* instance and *every* time thereafter. I will talk more about verbal abuse later.

Realistic Expectations

This may not sound like what you expected. Perhaps you expected that I would have examples where you agree and then your partner also becomes agreeable and nice. That is what will happen with partners who are basically nice—when there is not a hot topic. But, niceness is too much to expect when your relationship is already stressed and you suddenly start using the agreement method. Your partner is not familiar with that way of communicating, doesn't know how to do problem solving with you, and you have not yet built up your partner's respect with good boundaries.

If you were my client and you did your parts well (the "you" parts in the examples above), I would congratulate you for making a good start on a good relationship with your partner. I would encourage you to hang in there even if it didn't go so well. Change takes time as well as realistic expectations about how fast progress will be made. People don't expect to get into shape by working out one time at the gym, no matter how good the exercise is. Neither can you expect that you are going to find any method that will create a transformation in your relationship from the first few times you use it.

Now is a good time to help you know what expectations are realistic for using the method of agreement.

Ten realistic expectations for using the method of agreement:

1. Your partner will not change immediately, and that is ok.
2. Your partner will persist in his or her usual way of communicating with you, until he or she is sure that way will not work anymore. For some partners, this may take five times, and for others, it may take 25 times.
3. Your partner will escalate his or her behavior (make it worse than usual) in an attempt to pull you back to the old way of communicating.
4. Your partner will change from debate to problem solving if you are consistent and persistent.
5. Your partner will respect you more and more as you use good boundaries.
6. Your relationship will not become better until after you and your partner have had success at coming to win-win solutions using problem solving (see the problem solving chapter).
7. Although it is more natural to continue to debate your partner, it will lead to the downfall of your marriage or relationship.
8. The agreement method will become natural and easier as you use it repeatedly.

9. Your partner will appreciate your hard work on the relationship *after* it improves for the both of you.
10. You will make mistakes while you are learning. Everyone does.

Using Agreement to End Sexual Selfishness

Affairs are an extreme form of both relational and sexual selfishness and are covered in a different chapter. Here we will consider some lesser, but important kinds of sexual selfishness and how you can respond to your spouse, while using the method of agreement, and discussing sexual issues.

Sexual selfishness is related to the frequency of sex, the duration of sex, and the way that sex is done. The main characteristic is that one spouse is satisfied and one is not. That's not at all an unusual thing and doesn't need to be a bad thing if the satisfied spouse is willing to work on making the sex enjoyable for the other spouse. It is only when he or she is not willing to do that that I would consider the partner to be selfish.

Just as with other kinds of problems, and perhaps more so, clear communication is the best way to set about making sex more enjoyable for both of you. Failing to communicate clearly what you want is also a kind of selfishness. If your spouse does not know what would make you enjoy sex more, then he or she is less likely to do that, and as a result sex will be less than it could be for the both of you. If you verbally hold back, it could deprive both of you of more pleasure and a better relationship.

If you are embarrassed or shy about talking about sex, that is your problem, so be careful not to blame your partner for not guessing what you want. If, after you have clearly stated what you want, you get refusal from your partner, then comes the time to deal with the issue between the two of you. Again, let's compare some examples of fuzzy and clear communication.

Fuzzy:
"I want to have better sex and more often."

Clear:

"I want to have sex at least twice a week and for you to make me orgasm before you do (for a woman).

or

"I want to have sex at least twice a week and to also get oral sex from you at least two other times per week (for a man or woman)."

Fuzzy:

"I want sex to be more interesting."

Clear:

"I want to have sex with the lights on, dress like Superman, and you like Lois Lane."

If you can't bring yourself to say what you want, then write it on a piece of paper and pass it to your spouse. Or draw a picture, or point to a picture. The main thing is to be clear. Your request does not obligate your spouse in any way, but you are not likely to get what you don't ask for.

Now, let's consider some communication possibilities.

No disagreement:

Your partner agrees. Hardly anything else remains here except to go buy a Superman costume.

Disagreement #1: I'm satisfied, what's your problem?

SPOUSE: "I don't want to do that. It's too much work."
YOU: "I know that you are satisfied with the way that we have sex, and I am glad that

you enjoy it. I want our sex to be enjoyable
for you. I want to enjoy it, too."
SPOUSE: "You don't enjoy sex? You always
seem to."
YOU: "You are right, having sex with you is
part of our special time together. But, I
think I can make it even better for you."
SPOUSE: "How?"
YOU: "Well, let's talk together a little about
how sex could become an even better part of
our relationship." (Move to problem
solving).

Disagreement #2: I'm too tired. You're the
problem.
SPOUSE: "Look, I know you want to have sex
more often, but I'm too tired. You know I
have to ..."
YOU: 'Yes, you work really hard and I
appreciate it. I don't want to make you
more tired."
SPOUSE: "So, that's why we can't have sex
all the time."
YOU: "All the time would be too much for
me, too. Could we talk about some ways to
have a little more sex without tiring you out
more?"
SPOUSE: "No, I don't think so."
YOU: "It sounds like there are some other
reasons than just being tired."
SPOUSE: "Well, to tell you the truth, I don't
really enjoy having sex with you very much."

> *YOU: "Wow, I'm glad to hear you say that. It looks like we both agree that our sex could be better."*
> *SPOUSE: "Well, I'm not the problem, you are."*
> *YOU: "Oh, good, it sounds like you are ready to start working on this right now. Let me grab a pencil and paper."*

The spouse's attempt to avoid talking about sex by blaming has totally not worked here. The way that you would be able to actually do this is by not focusing on winning, being right, or changing your spouse. A good goal here is to understand the underlying issues for your spouse. Don't treat this as blaming if you are the one seeking answers. Use his or her reason as part of the brainstorming process.

Disagreement #3: You're a sicko!

> *SPOUSE: "You are sick! How could you even suggest such a thing? You need to see a doctor and get your head shrunk or something."*
> *YOU: "That could be, but thank you for listening to me, anyhow. I want to be able to tell you what I want and listen to what you want, even when we disagree."*
> *SPOUSE: "I'm never going to do what you want no matter how many times we talk about it."*
> *YOU: "That is really good to know and I'm glad you made that clear. Could we talk about some other possibilities that might be more acceptable to you?"*
> *SPOUSE: "Well, I don't know. I'm still shook up about your last idea."*

> **YOU:** *"Yes, now might not be a good time.*
> *Could we try again tomorrow?"*
> **SPOUSE:** *"I guess so."*

The spouse in this example is obviously much more sexually conservative. One spouse usually is. The way the spouse reacts does not need to lead to defensiveness, arguing, or withdrawal. Many people would be tempted to withdraw here after receiving such a moral judgment. The best goal here is helping your spouse to feel comfortable talking about things rather than to defend yourself for having "sick" ideas.

Remember, if this way of talking works for your spouse to shut you up and get you to withdraw, he or she can use a very similar response to any idea you have about anything (travel, buying a home, etc.). Righteous indignation is just another form of attack and avoidance.

No Communication Taboos

Communicating about sex should not be taboo for couples who are already having sex. Learning how to dialogue about it, and to be sensitive to each other's needs and desires is an important part of making sure your relationship stays strong. Couples who don't talk about sex with each other may nevertheless have affairs and talk about it with lovers. Make it your goal to be able to talk with your spouse more easily about sex than his or her lover would. It is not a "thought crime" for you or your spouse to talk about your desires.

Using Agreement to End Time Selfishness

If your partner is spending most or all of his or her free time doing things only for himself or herself, that is selfish. It wouldn't be if he or she were single, but you are in a committed relationship. Without spending quality time together, there is not much meaning for your relationship. Just like selfishness with money or sex, your partner is going to be more interested in justifying himself or herself than he or she will be in making things more fair, time-wise.

As a positive communicator, your job will be to stay away from the "who is right" debate over the correct use of time. Having to present evidence that your partner should spend more time with you would be a sad thing. A better goal would be to turn this into a win-win situation by helping your partner enjoy being with you more, as it probably was early in your relationship.

As before, you need to start with clear, not fuzzy, communication.

Fuzzy:
> *"I would like us to spend more time together."*

Clear:
> *"I would like us to spend an hour a day doing something together other than watching TV and also to go out on a date once a week."*

Fuzzy:
> *"I wish you wouldn't spend so much time on the computer."*

Clear:
> *"I want you to take a walk with me after dinner every day."*

Fuzzy:
> *"I wish I were as important to you as your friends are."*

Clear:
> *"I want you to take me out at least as often as you go out with your friends."*

I think it's important to see in these examples that the goal is not to stop your partner from doing what he or she enjoys doing.

If you tried to directly limit his or her time on the computer or with friends, you are likely to have a head-on confrontation with him, which could end up making your situation worse. As before, your partner does not have to agree. These clear communications are not points to debate. They are messages to your partner about what you want so that he or she has a chance to give you what you want—without having to guess what you want. Making our partners "guess" is a problem which resides in us, and not in our partners.

Now, let's consider some objections from your partner and how you might deal with them using the agreement method.

Objection #1: I spend enough time with you already

> **PARTNER:** *"I already spend a lot of time with you."*
>
> **YOU:** *"It's true that we are both here at the same time. But, I would like to have more one on one time with you because you are my teddy bear."*
>
> **PARTNER:** *"Well, I work hard all day and I want to do my things. I need to relax."*
>
> **YOU:** *"You sure are a hard worker. I really appreciate all that you do. Maybe we could figure out some ways to be together more and you still have time to do your activities."*
>
> **PARTNER:** *"I don't see how."*
>
> **YOU:** *"I don't see how, either. I think we need to do a little thinking. If it isn't possible, then I could understand better and not need to ask you about it again."*
>
> **PARTNER:** *"That would be good. I get tired of being bugged about it."*

YOU: "Good. You agree. Then let me get a piece of paper and we can put our heads together."

There are multiple openings here for starting a fight. Your refusal to do so does not put you in a one down position. It does help you to get to problem solving, where real change can happen. One of the worst aspects of the debate or argument method is that it prevents problem solving.

Let's consider another objection.

Objection #2: My time is not your business

PARTNER: "I will go out with my friends as often as I want and you won't tell me otherwise."

YOU: "You are sure right about that. I don't need to tell you how to use your time. And, it's up to you whether you spend time with your friends or not."

PARTNER: "You never liked my friends. You are always jealous of them, because you don't have any friends of your own."

YOU: "You're right, I don't have as many close friends as you."

PARTNER: "Well, you should make some instead of expecting me to stay home with you all the time."

YOU: "You're right. Expecting you to stay home all the time wouldn't be a good solution. Although I want to spend more time with you, I do agree that I could use more friends."

PARTNER: "Well, make some. I'm not stopping you."

> *YOU: "No, you're not. You are really good at making friends. Would you help me to figure out some ways to make some friends?"*

This scenario might make you think that your partner has successfully avoided spending more time with you. But, what you need to see is that you are getting to the point of your partner working together with you to help you. It is a positive step in your relationship although it doesn't immediately get what you want. The more you and your partner work together positively like this, the more he or she will want to spend time with you. So, it does help to get what you originally wanted (more time with your partner). Progress usually does not come in one step.

Let's try one more objection with an even tougher partner.

Objection #3: The angry bear

> *PARTNER: "To hell with that. I'm doing what I want and I don't need any suggestions from you."*
>
> *YOU: "Thanks for making that really clear. It helps."*
>
> *PARTNER: "Huh? How does THAT help?"*
>
> *YOU: "Well, I know that I need to do something else with my time other than to expect you to do things with me."*
>
> *PARTNER: "What is THAT supposed to mean? You don't want to do things with me?"*
>
> *YOU: "Not if you don't want to."*
>
> *PARTNER: "Well, maybe I do."*
>
> *YOU: "Ok, tell you what. When you want to do things with me, let me know. Otherwise, I will plan to do things without you."*

PARTNER: "I don't like the sound of that."
YOU: "Yes, I know it's not ideal. But, I love
you and I want our relationship to work."

What you can see in this example is a really controlling partner who is used to getting his or her way through power. In this example, you don't oppose that power, but neither do you agree to just sit around and wait for your partner to be available. You make your desire to be together clear. You make your love clear. But, you also make clear that you will have other things to do. This is a good example of combining a loving message with boundaries. Persist this way and your partner's power plays will no longer work—which will put you on an equal level. Quite a change just by being agreeable, don't you think?!

When Things Get Better

The examples that I gave you above illustrate what it is like to start using this method with a partner who is used to either arguing, shutting you up, or shutting you down. It's the kind of difficult partner that I wrote about in my book, *What to Do When He Won't Change*, but in this case could be either a man or a woman. I intentionally gave you these kinds of very difficult examples because I want you to see that you can use this method in the most difficult of situations, except where there is verbal or physical abuse (for which neither arguing nor agreeing will be helpful). If you can learn to use this method in difficult situations, then using it in less difficult situations will be a breeze.

If you can persist in using this method as illustrated with the difficult types of people in the examples above, they *will* change. They have to. Because their way of talking will no longer work for them. And that is your real goal—to shut down the way of talking about problems which is not really talking at all. To change disagreement to collaboration and get to win-win. Because it is only with collaboration and win-win that the problems will get resolved and your relationship will get stronger.

Let me give you an example of what will happen if you persist in using this method with such a difficult partner.

Example: Persistence pays off

> PARTNER: *"You never listen to me."*
> YOU: *"I might not be doing a good job of listening. Let's do some problem solving about it, to make it better for both of us."*
> PARTNER: *"Ok."*

I kid you not. Your partner will come to like this method of problem solving because it gets your partner unstuck, too. It helps your partner to do something that he or she was not able to do before—to effectively work out differences. And, your partner will also like it because it gets him or her more of what he or she wants. Remember, people continue to do what they have had success with, and their older, less successful ways drop out.

If you have a more easygoing partner, this method will be very easy to use and from the beginning will be much more like the three line example above. Even so, you will need to be familiar with problem solving so that you can do it with your partner. The problem solving chapter gives you an easy, step by step method for doing that.

When You Slip Up

What happens if you lose it—if you slip back to old ways of arguing, defending, or attacking? Your partner will immediately slip back, too. It will be a fall-back position for the both of you. When you slip up, you need to see it as just that—a slip up. It's not a failure. You haven't lost all you have gained. You just got off track and need to get back on. Here is an example of this:

> PARTNER: *"You never listen to me."*
> YOU: *"What do you mean? I always listen to you."*
> PARTNER: *"Ok, then tell me what I told you last night after dinner."*
> YOU: *"I don't remember."*

> *PARTNER: "See, you never listen to me. If you did, you would remember what I said..."*
> *(At this point, you can feel the argument building and recognize it as the old way of fighting about problems instead of resolving them).*
> *YOU: "Wait, wait. I'm sorry, I'm losing it, and I don't want to. I want us to get along."*
> *PARTNER: "Well then, you need to listen to me when I talk to you instead of thinking about what happened on your TV show."*
> *YOU: "I might not be doing a good job of listening. Let's do some problem solving about it, to make it better for both of us."*
> *PARTNER: "Ok."*

Notice in this example, that when you slip up, you don't blame your partner for that. Blame is part of debating or arguing. It doesn't belong in the agreement method. In the agreement method your goal is neither to be right nor wrong, but simply to get to collaboration. It is in the process of problem solving where you will experience your "win" and where your partner will also experience his or her "win."

Summary

The agreement method can be used with very difficult partners, but cannot be used with verbal or physical abuse. It is not a "quick fix" method for ailing relationships, but if used consistently it does have the ability to improve the way you communicate. The goal of the agreement method is to quickly get you and your partner to the point of collaboration, or more specifically, to the point of problem solving. Just as with other kinds of communication, it is important to have good boundaries.

It is the combination of: 1) good boundaries, 2) good communication, 3) loving messages, and 4) collaborative problem solving which has the greatest potential for turning a failing marriage or relationship into a close one.

USING AGREEMENT TO END PARENTING CONFLICTS

Arguing with your spouse about the best way to raise children is not an effective way to become a better parent. Not only that, but the arguing weakens the bond between you and your spouse, which also makes things worse for your children. One of the very best things that you can do to ensure a well adjusted child is to have a strong marital bond with your spouse. The method of agreement can help you to have that.

You and your spouse were raised in different homes (hopefully!) and will have some differing opinions about the best way to parent. Some of your opinions will be based on what worked well and didn't work well in your family of origin. All parents want to do better for their children than their parents did for them.

Your Child Is Not You

What I would like to suggest to you is that your child is not the same as you were when you were a child. What was best for you might not be best for your child. Your child has his or her own temperament, personality, intelligence, and skills. Also, your child is growing up in a different world than you did. He or she needs to be prepared to live in a different world than you prepared for. Even if your child had the exact same environment as you did, your child would still be different from you in many ways. So, do not be quick to decide that you intuitively know what is best for your child.

The best attitude to have about your own parenting opinions is "I think that such and such would be good, but I am not 100% sure. I need to explore all the options before making up my mind." Having a mind that is at least a little bit open will help you to listen to your partner's ideas instead of just right away assuming that you know best and that whatever your spouse has to say doesn't count. This is true even if you have a PhD in child development. Even if you are right, and do know better, by keeping an open mind you will have a chance of helping your partner to make the best informed choices as well. You can't forget about your marriage or relationship just because you have a child.

Keep in mind that you selected your spouse from among all the other possible candidates. That means that although your spouse is different from you, he or she has some characteristics that you admire and are attracted to. If you can combine the best parts of your spouse and the best parts of yourself in your child, you will end up with a child who surpasses you. And, isn't that what every parent wants?

How do you promote a strong marital bond when you and your spouse disagree on what's best for your child? There are several ways to resolve such an impasse. Perhaps the easiest way, and best way, is for you and your spouse to get the advice of experts—either by reading books, attending classes, or by meeting with a pediatrician or child psychologist. After getting the information, you and your partner will still be the ones to make the decisions, but at least they will be well informed decisions.

Types of Conflict in Parenting

There are many kinds of conflicts that can occur in parenting over the lifespan of children. Even elderly parents can have conflicts about what is best for their middle aged children! What I will do in this chapter is to teach you the general method for resolving differences between you and your child's mother or father. I say it that way because many parents are not married to each other or won't be by the time their child is grown. Nevertheless, they need to be able to talk about parenting issues.

Working collaboratively with your child's mother or father has many benefits for you and for your child. It certainly takes a lot of stress out of parenting. For your child's sake, do not put your child in the middle of yourself and your spouse or ex-spouse. Don't make your child a messenger, don't try to damage your child's relationship with his or her other parent, and don't ask your child to decide which parent has made the better decision. All of these things hurt your child. You can help to ensure this doesn't happen by working collaboratively with your child's other parent, regardless of your opinion of his or her ability as a father or mother.

Throughout this chapter, I will say "spouse" or "partner," although your child's other parent may not be your spouse or your partner. It is just less clumsy to say it this way than to say, "your child's other parent." And, for the majority of readers, spouse or partner is close enough. The material also applies to step-parents. Step-parents differ a lot in terms of their authority and role in their step-child's life. The younger the child, the more a step-parent is going to fill the same role as a biological parent or adoptive parent.

Step-parents can also have conflicts with their partner's ex-spouses. The agreement method will work equally well for them.

Alternatives to Agreement

Before you begin to consider the agreement method, take a moment to consider your alternatives. As you will find, if you have a good idea, it is helpful to have people consider the *alternatives* to your idea. Then, your idea will seem so much the better. As much as I could tell you how great the agreement method is for resolving parental differences, it will benefit you to first consider how debate, authority, and compromise might work for you.

The good old fashioned way of making decisions

The traditional way for parents to make decisions is by discussion and debate (argument). Each parent presents his or her opinions and reasons. The more different the opinions and the more emotionally invested each parent is in them, the hotter the debate will run. But, if one person has reasons that are obviously better than the other person, then discussion and even a little debate may work.

When there are strong differences of opinion, typically couples argue about what to do, then both retreat for a while and consider what has been said. If the parents are both fairly reasonable and the solution more or less obvious, the person with the weaker argument will back down. "I thought about it some more and I think you are right." One of the biggest problems with this method is that only two possibilities are considered—what your partner believes is best and what you believe is best. Also, unlike the agreement method, there is no backup plan in case things go wrong. Because one person's decision gets followed, if things go badly, usually that person gets blamed. Also, debate does not have the feel of co-parenting. This is especially true if the same parent tends to win the debates more often.

Having one parent in charge

Authority can work well if the person with the power to make the decisions is actually better at making decisions. One model of using authority is to have each parent be in charge of different areas of decision making, according to how knowledgeable he or she is about such things. One parent can make education decisions, for example, while the other parent makes health decisions. One parent can make clothes decisions while the other parent makes sports decisions. In areas where neither parent has expertise (or where they both do), other methods of decision making can be used, such as debate, agreement, professional consultation, or compromise.

The method of compromise

Compromise, on the surface, sounds like a good way to make decisions because each person gains something and each person loses something. Certainly there is a kind of fairness with compromise. But, will compromise result in the best decisions for your child? Or will compromise result in watered-down decisions for your child? Say, for example that one of you wants to send your child to sports camp for two weeks and the other parent thinks it would be better to spend the money on a family vacation. Would a good compromise be to take a weekend vacation and send your child to a cheaper camp for one week? Maybe, maybe not. Because compromise usually results in worse options and gradually increasing resentment, I consider compromise to be one of the last methods to use for resolving differences. It should be used only after all better methods have failed.

The Last Resort

There is one more method which is even worse than compromise. It is *agreeing to disagree*. Agreeing to disagree, in my opinion, is a last resort method of handling differences— particularly where the welfare of your child is concerned. It results in parents who continue to be in conflict and puts off decisions that are important for your child. If things get to this point, then I recommend you get professional help.

Parenting Together without Conflict

The same decisions that can be reached by the methods of authority, debate, and compromise, can be reached with the method of agreement The added advantages of the method of agreement are that there is no need for conflict, more possible solutions are considered, and there is a backup plan in case things go wrong. Additionally, parents will have a unified and more loving front. Loving, cooperative, and unified parents contribute a lot to a child's healthy emotional development. The work that you do with your spouse now can save your child years of work later.

Your child learns mainly by watching what you do and how you do it. Because of that, your child does not learn how to be a child from you. Your child learns how to be a spouse and a parent from you. It is not only the decisions you make that affect your child, but also the way you make those decisions.

As I will reiterate throughout this book, the agreement method is not used as a one step method. We can't simply agree with someone and presto, the problem is solved. Rather, we use agreement to begin the process of problem solving (see the chapter on problem solving). We also maintain good boundaries to protect ourselves, our partners, and (in the case of parenting), our child, from harm.

When there is emotional or physical abuse to ourselves, we never use the agreement method. Also, when there is emotional or physical abuse to our child we don't use the agreement method. Emotional and physical safety come first. If you believe your child is being emotionally or physically abused, seek professional help (counselors, hospital, police, child abuse hotline, etc.) as soon as it is safe to do so. Then, keep yourself and your child safe until you get the help you need.

Ask Good Questions

In earlier chapters, I suggested that a good way to start to get more of what you want is to make a clear request, so that your partner can understand exactly what it is you want. You express your desires so that your partner doesn't have to guess them or be blamed for not guessing them. Such requests are either going to bring agreement or disagreement from your partner. If disagreement, you can then use the method of agreement to promote a cooperative way to find solutions.

You can also use clear statements when discussing desires that you have for your child, or when you have a preferred way of dealing with your child. This is not a bad way, but in a moment I will show you an even better way.

Example clear communication about a parenting desire:
"I would like to send John Jr. to private school X so that he can be well prepared for college."

This is a bit closed ended for coming to a mutual agreement about your child. It seems you have already come to a decision about what to do without discussing it with your spouse. If I want something for myself, then yes, I need to say clearly what that is. But, if I want to *share* an important decision about our child, then I would prefer that we come up with some ideas together. If my spouse is stumped for ideas or has no preference, then I will suggest some of my own ideas.

Instead of a clear communication, you can use questions to open up discussion about a parenting topic. Here are two good questions that you can use for almost any situation or occasion:

Using questions instead of clear communications:
"What do you think about ...?" or
"What are your concerns about...?"

Take for example, the topic of where to send your child to school. Instead of saying, "I think we should send John Jr. to private school x," you can say, "We need to make a decision about where to send John Jr. to school. What do you think about it?" If this leads to differences of opinion, you can then use the method of agreement and problem solving to arrive at the best decision for your child.

How to Agree with an Unreasonable Partner

Since this is a chapter about parenting conflicts, let's assume that your partner gives you an idea that you think is absurd.

Maybe your partner says, "I think it would be best for you to give up your career for the next 12 years and home school John Jr., because home schooled kids outperform kids who go to school." It's easy for you to guess how an argument could come of this, so I don't need to go there.

With the agreement method, you pick out the part of what your spouse is saying that you agree with and ignore the rest. Assuming that you don't like the idea of giving up your career, you might say, "Yes, I think it would be great if John Jr. can outperform his peers. I want him to have the best, too." Have you agreed that you will home school John Jr.? No. You really haven't agreed to do anything. What you are doing is finding a point of connection with your spouse which you can then build on.

Example: Using agreement to prevent conflict over parenting differences

> *SPOUSE: "I think it would be best for you to give up your career for the next 12 years and home school John Jr., because home schooled kids outperform kids who go to school."*
> *YOU: "Yes, I think it would be great if John Jr. can outperform his peers. I want him to have the best, too."*
> *SPOUSE: "Good, then we are agreed that you will quit your job when the time comes."*
> *YOU: "Before we agree to that, would you help me to look at our options on paper so that I can feel it really is the best option for us?"*
> *SPOUSE: "I guess so."*

What comes next is problem solving. You will both be coming up with a definition of the problem which could start out like this:

"What would be the best way for John Jr. to be prepared for college?"

Which could then be tweaked like this,

"What would be the best way for John Jr. to be prepared for college, while still keeping our relationship strong?"

Since a strong parental relationship goes along with good parenting, it should be acceptable to your partner to formulate the problem this way. (If you don't know what I am talking about in formulating a problem, you need to go back and read the chapter on problem solving).

Once you have clearly and positively formulated the problem, you both will then brainstorm options for how to prepare John Jr., and will also talk about the pros and cons of each option. By the time you are done, your spouse and you will have considered many aspects related to home schooling as well as other options. You may never need to disagree with your spouse's idea because in going over the pros and cons, it may become obvious to your spouse that home schooling is not the best idea in your son's case. On the other hand, your spouse may help you to consider many positives about home schooling that you didn't think of. Either way, you end up with a joint decision and a backup plan that you both feel good about. All without disagreeing even once. When it comes time to tell John Jr. about the school plans for him, you and your spouse will have a unified front.

Example: Using agreement with an unreasonable spouse

YOU: "Before we agree to that, would you help me to look at our options on paper so that I can feel it really is the best option for us?"

SPOUSE: "No, my mind is made up, what I decided is what is going to happen."
YOU: "Unless I feel it is the best decision, I won't be quitting my job. Then, if you want John Jr. to be home schooled, you will have to be the one to do it."
SPOUSE: "You never want to do what is best or to follow my opinion..."
YOU: "I'm not going to argue with you. If you change your mind about looking at our options on paper, let me know."

My guess is that if your partner does not want to do this on paper and consider the options, then your partner already thinks that his or her idea is very weak. People who are confident of their ideas usually don't mind going over the costs and benefits of those ideas.

Example conflict about how to discipline your teen

Let's suppose that your teen does something that has to be addressed. In this example, we will consider that your teen was supposed to be home by 11:00 pm, but did not come home until 6:00 a.m. the next morning. The reason, your teen says, is because her watch was broken and she didn't realize how late it was until the sun was coming up. You have told your daughter that you will discuss it with your spouse and then you will both deal with this situation later.

Although you might think that you need to do something right away, your teen is no longer in any danger and your nerves are likely to be shot. Doing some problem solving with your spouse about what to do will help you both to be reasonable and effective, and even more importantly, to have a backup plan in case the situation continues. Having a backup plan has saved more than one parent from going to the loony bin (otherwise known as the funny farm). Let's imagine the conversation with your spouse:

> **YOU:** *"What are we going to do about Susan staying out all night and not even calling us?"*
> **SPOUSE:** *"Well, I know what I'm going to do. I'm not going to let her go out again for the rest of the year."*
> **YOU:** *"Well, that would be one way for her to understand how serious this is. But, let's look at <u>all</u> of our options on paper before we decide."*
> **SPOUSE:** *"Ok, but it's not going to make a difference."*
> **YOU:** *"You may be right. Let's just make sure."*

Notice in this example that you don't say whether you agree or disagree with your spouse. You also don't say what your idea is (if you have any). But, you play a very important role in getting to problem solving, where you and your spouse can consider the long term implications of your decisions. By the time you and your spouse go through the problem solving steps, you are both likely to have an entirely different solution to this problem. And, you will have a backup plan as well.

Example conflict about whether to use day care

Suppose a mother wants to use day care for her child so she can return to work. Her husband argues that day care is a bad idea because it is expensive and will cost almost as much as the mother will earn. Both parents have some good points, but are arguing different aspects of the situation—an apples and oranges kind of argument. The husband decides to use the agreement method to stop the arguing.

> **Wife:** *"I think I should go back to work. Have you tried staying in this house seven days a week?!"*

Husband: "Yes, I think that would be difficult for me to do. I can see how it would be hard for you."

Wife: "You see? That's why I should go back to work."

Husband: "I guess that would be one possible solution. Can we sit down and make sure it's the best solution before we decide to go that way?"

Wife: "I'm not going to change my mind, no matter how much we talk about it."

Husband: "I can see that. But, it might make me feel better about your decision if we can compare it to the other choices."

Wife: "Well, the other choice is to stay home and I'm not going to do that."

Husband: "Believe me, I'm not going to make you. Now, come here honey, and sit down. Let me get a piece of paper and we can look at this together."

Wife: (says nothing).

Husband: (Holds out his hand for her and waits patiently until she takes it).

Wife: (After some hesitation, takes his hand).

Husband: "Let's get some coffee."

Wife: "Ok."

In this example, an argument is developing. Both people have their temper up and the husband is the first to realize that they aren't getting anywhere. It's not too late for him to use the agreement method, but he will have to persist gently for awhile before his wife will be calm enough to sit down and do problem solving with him. The husband uses physical touch to reconnect and wisely suggests getting a cup of coffee to take the focus away from their argument. After they get their coffee, the husband will take out a piece of paper and start the positive, problem solving process with his wife.

Troubleshooting

There are many possible varieties of parenting conflicts and many potential outcomes. Because of that you are sure to come across situations where the agreement method just does not seem to work at all. I have not maintained that the agreement method can be used for everything. What I have maintained is that most of the time it works better than debate/argument, and usually works better than authority or compromise. There will be times when authority is needed, especially in cases of abuse, custody, and visitation. And there will be times when compromise is the best way, especially when you and your child's other parent can't come to an agreement.

Below, I have tried to anticipate some questions you may have about using the method of agreement with parenting. Also, some of your other questions may actually be answered elsewhere in this book. If you have not done so, it is important that you read the chapter on the agreement method and the chapter on problem solving before beginning to use these skills for sharing parenting decisions.

"This is hard to do because I am so upset at the time of disagreement."

That is to be expected. It is not easy to be upset and do a rational process. Being upset and doing an irrational process like attacking and defending is much easier, but also much less productive. To get better at talking with your partner, your kids, or anyone whom you have conflict with, you first need to work on calming down. For some people that will mean taking a time out.

If you hear something you disagree with strongly, you can excuse yourself and take a little walk around the block or have a cup of tea. Calm your breathing and remind yourself that your partner is not out to start world war three. He or she is just saying what he or she thinks is best. Although you know that he or she is wrong, the best thing for you to do is to agree on *something* so that you can get to the problem solving process. Then, your partner will convince himself or herself that another solution will actually be better. You don't need to instantly react to your emotions.

"This is hard to do because my partner is upset when I suggest we sit down and work on things."

Your partner is likely to be upset if you argue before using this method. This will happen especially when you are first learning to use the agreement method. The better you get at it though, the sooner you will use it—avoiding argument and upset. If your partner is already upset, you need to judge how upset *you* are.

If you are calm, you can do what the husband did in the example in the previous section. Become agreeable and loving, take a little break with your partner, and then begin the problem solving on a positive note.

At other times though, especially when you are also upset, it will be better for you both to take separate breaks to calm down. After you have done that, think about something you can really agree with your partner about and go to him or her with that. Don't re-present your own solution until you are in step two of the problem solving. Otherwise, you run the risk of recreating an argument.

"Do you tell your child about the backup plan?"

In most cases, it will be helpful to tell an *older* child that you have a backup plan in case things don't go well. The number one reason for that is to help children to work with you rather than against you. For example, a child may intentionally flunk out of private school to get back to public school with his or her friends. But, knowing that home schooling is the backup plan may motivate your child to do well with the first plan. If you decide that your daughter's dates need to be chaperoned, she may sneak off for her private dates, but may not if the backup plan is a juvenile detention facility.

With young children it may be best not to tell them about a backup plan, as it may be confusing or more upsetting to them.

"What if I can't come to an agreement with my spouse?"

If you can't come to an agreement via the problem solving method, you certainly won't come to an agreement by arguing. My recommendation is to then use an authority who you both respect to help make the decision. But don't just simply have the authority tell you what to do. Go over the options that you have considered in the problem solving process. If there is no such person that you both respect to help you with the decision, you may need a consultation session or two with a child psychologist. Unless your child has psychological problems, it probably won't be necessary for your child to see the psychologist.

"What if we can't find a good solution?"

There are no perfect solutions for anyone, anytime, anywhere. We all do the best we can and then deal with the consequences. That goes for rocket scientists, governments, and parents alike. However, if your solutions are all bad, then it is time to get professional help. The most helpful thing about professionals is they can more accurately gauge what is actually going to work, and they usually have a lot more ideas about what to do.

Summary

Arguing (debating) is a particularly bad method of resolving parenting conflicts because it sets a poor example for your child. Also, debate is *less* likely to result in your having a unified front. Children are very sensitive to disagreement between their parents. Not being unified can set up a good parent/bad parent dichotomy in their mind. This will never be helpful to your child—even when you are the one your child sees as "good."

The agreement method has the added benefits of allowing for other possible solutions as well as the creation of a backup plan. Simply having a backup plan can bring peace of mind to parenting.

I have absolutely no pleasure in the stimulants in which I sometimes so madly indulge. It has not been in the pursuit of pleasure that I have periled life and reputation and reason. It has been the desperate attempt to escape from torturing memories, from a sense of insupportable loneliness and a dread of some strange impending doom.

Edgar Allan Poe
American Author & Poet

♥6♥

USING AGREEMENT WHEN YOUR SPOUSE HAS A DRUG OR ALCOHOL ADDICTION

Arguing about your spouse's drug or alcohol abuse won't help. Arguing will just create more distance in your relationship and make it more difficult to talk about the substance abuse. The stress of arguing may even give the substance abuser one more excuse to abuse substances.

Substance abusers generally do not become motivated to work on overcoming their abuse until they experience severe negative consequences from the abuse. If you argue, they won't see it as the drugs or alcohol causing problems, but as *you* causing problems. For arguing to be effective, it would have to be so severe that it would damage your relationship in the process. If your spouse is abusing drugs or alcohol, do not even consider debating (arguing) about it. Put any anger you have to better use by using more effective, less harmful methods.

Sometimes it may *seem* like arguing helps, but that's because something effective got mixed in with the arguing. For example, if you argue a lot and say that you are separating or filing for divorce, it may have a strong impact. What is important to see here is that it wasn't the arguing that caused the impact—it was the threat of separation. If you were calm and made the same threat, it would have had even more impact.

Arguing, combined with boundaries, is effective only because of the boundaries. *Agreement* combined with boundaries is even more effective, and doesn't damage relationships. If you have difficulty setting boundaries without getting angry, it is time for you to change. It isn't necessary to be angry to help others to change harmful behaviors, whether they are your kids, friends, coworkers, or spouse.

The right combination of actions for helping a substance abusing spouse is to maintain a good emotional connection while also using good boundaries. You may need to separate or divorce if things are really bad. But if you maintain an emotional connection with your spouse, he or she will be motivated to work on overcoming the abuse and on saving the relationship. There is a difference between separating because you want to help your spouse and separating because you can't stand your spouse. The first is helping; the second is running away.

People who have chronically abused drugs or alcohol may have experienced many rejections in their life. If you simply reject such a person, it probably won't make much difference as far as their substance abuse goes. What is likely to make a difference is a tough love approach, which they probably have not encountered before. People who have rejected them probably were tough, but not loving. Being tough is not the same as tough love.

Some people confuse a "tough love" approach with a "tough" approach. Tough love is actually a combination of being tough *and* being loving. Simply being tough won't do it. Simply being loving won't do it, either. To give your spouse the experience of tough love, you must maintain your verbal messages of love and desire for connection, even as you use tough boundaries. Contrast the following three messages:

Tough message:
"I'm moving out of here because I can't stand your drinking and selfish behaviors anymore."

Loving message:
  "I love you and want to be with you no matter what."
Tough love message:
  "I love you and want to be with you, but I can't while you are drinking. It hurts too much."

The first message is tough, but it is not loving. The boundary used is separation. The second is loving, but lacks a boundary, resulting in acceptance of the substance abuse. The third has both a loving message and a boundary of separation. The tough message is blaming. The loving message is needy. The tough love message is neither blaming nor needy.

The tough love message does not point the finger of blame. It says, "I want," "I can't," and "I'm going to." This is taking responsibility—the opposite of blame. *I* will do something because this situation is no good for *me.* The tough love message is harder to say when we are angry and hurt, but our love and commitment to our spouse demands that we not intentionally do them harm. We may have to leave them, but we don't have to kick them at the same time.

Having a tough and loving approach doesn't mean waiting until you are ready to move out and then saying such a thing. Tough love means being consistently tough and loving as long as you are together. Tough love promotes the relationship while keeping people safe. As you will see, the method of agreement, when combined with good boundaries, is ideal for effectively loving and helping a partner who is addicted to a substance.

Conflicts with Partners Who Abuse Substances

Couples who have to deal with the issue of substance abuse also have to deal with all of the other aspects of relationships and running a home. They are not likely to have conflict just over the abuse. Finances, child rearing, sex, work, and socialization conflicts are likely to not only be present, but are probably made even worse because of the substance abuse. In such cases, the most appropriate place to focus your energy is on dealing with the substance abuse. It is hardly possible to fix the other problems in your relationship while the substance abuse remains.

This is not a chicken and egg question because financial and other stressors do not cause substance abuse. They may be used as an excuse to abuse drugs or alcohol, but they did not cause the drug or alcohol problem. Most people who have these stresses do not go on to abuse substances. On the other hand, drug and alcohol problems can *cause* financial, health, social, legal, and other problems. To get to the root of the problems, you need to deal with the substance abuse.

The most common conflicts related to substance abuse are conflicts about:

1. The substance abuser continuing to use drugs or alcohol.
2. The substance abuser not keeping promises to reduce or stop the substance abuse.
3. Violence, verbal abuse, and threats from the substance abuser, especially when under the influence of the substance.
4. Dissatisfaction with the emotional and intimate relationship.
5. Job loss, financial problems, and inappropriate use of money.
6. The substance abuser's social isolation or association only with other substance abusers.

The most common mistakes of partners of people who abuse substances are:

1. Abusing drugs or alcohol to connect with their substance abusing partner.
2. Making excuses for their partner's substance abuse.
3. Denying how serious the substance abuse problem is.
4. Allowing verbal and/or physical abuse or threats.

These are all mistakes because they contribute to the continuation of the problem and the deterioration of the relationship. They do not help the substance abuser. Although they may feel "patient" or "loving," actually they are codependent and damaging.

Focus on the Future

When you have a relationship with either a lot of problems or one big problem, the obvious place to start seems to be focusing on the problems. In practice though, that is *not* a good place to start. Since substance abusers tend to avoid problems, focusing on them just increases avoidance. He or she can do that by either trying to shut you down (shut you up), or by physically getting away from you. If you do manage to corner your partner somehow, you could end up getting hurt. At the very least you are likely to get into a shouting match or to get into arguing about every subject other than the one that you really wanted to talk about. Like picking up a wet bar of soap, the harder you squeeze, the further he or she will fly from you.

A better place to start is with the end in mind. This is one of the major differences between relationship coaching and relationship counseling. In relationship coaching, we focus on where we want to go and what we want to achieve rather than on how the problems got started in the first place. The benefit of a forward looking approach is that it allows each person to focus on what he or she wants and what he or she needs to do to contribute to that happening. It also allows people to make back up plans in case what they want to happen doesn't.

Typical coaching questions are "What would you like your life to be like in five years?" "If it couldn't be that way, what's a second choice that would be ok?" "What obstacles are in the way of getting that?" "What can you do to overcome or get around those obstacles?" The substance abuser, like everyone else, needs to have hope for the future in order to have motivation to change.

Make a Backup Plan

When you have a substance abusing spouse, your backup plan is vital. Plan A may be for your spouse to stop abusing substances. Plan B will be what you are going to do if the substance abuse doesn't stop. Having such a Plan B will help you to feel secure enough to follow through with your tough love approach. Without a Plan B, you may fear losing your relationship so much that you become codependent for the substance abuse.

When you have a Plan B, you will have a much stronger stand in front of your spouse. Without a Plan B your spouse will sense that you have no choice but to stay with him or her, regardless of the substance abuse. Although you don't want to end your relationship, you need to have a possible way out of the relationship. This is particularly true if you need to give your spouse the choice between you and the bottle (powder, syringe, pills, or whatever). If you give such a choice, but you are not prepared to leave, you would lose respect and damage your relationship more. Boundaries are never empty threats. They are actions you are *prepared* to take.

Where Can You Agree?

It's important that you never agree with your spouse that using substances to deal with problems is a good thing. For the substance abuser, it's not a good thing. It's not the same as most people having a glass of wine to relax a little. Substance abusers are using a toxin to create a biological and mental state that they can't feel right without. This toxin destroys their mind and body, impairs their functioning, and hurts others around them.

Your substance abusing partner actually has more in common with you than he or she has differences. Although he or she may not actually do so well, he would like to. Although he may at times push you away, he doesn't want you to go away. No one likes rejection and abandonment—even when their behaviors contribute to other people doing just that. So, the best place for you to agree is with your desire to have a close relationship. You can also agree that overcoming substance abuse is hard and takes time.

It is not necessary to get your partner to agree to quit the substance abuse. That would be a big burden to put on you. You only need to focus on presenting loving messages while also creating an environment of safety for yourself and the right boundaries. You need to work on giving your partner a choice between getting your help and losing you. You also need to stay loving. When you give tough and loving messages, your partner is much more likely to accept your help—after you put your boundaries in place. Although it won't be easy, it will give you and your partner an opportunity for an intimate relationship that you probably won't be able to have if the substance abuse continues.

Agreement Alone Won't Stop Substance Abuse

Making all the changes that are necessary and educating you in all the information you need for a substance abuse intervention is beyond the scope of this book. You can get other books entirely on that subject, and I suggest that you do. If possible, when you are ready to begin addressing this issue, find a counselor for yourself. I recommend you find a drug and alcohol counselor, even though you are not the one with the abuse problem. The substance abuse counselor will be able to connect you with the right resources in your area and will help you to have the best chance for helping your spouse. You need to be more educated about this than your partner, both to help your partner and to decrease the chance that you are going to be misled by false information from your partner.

Although this chapter is not enough, I think it will still help you learn a few important things. First, it is my hope that you discover that fighting with your partner is not only not helpful, it is harmful. Second, the real leverage you have in helping your partner to change is the boundaries you set (which the counselor should help you with). And third, you can and should, still give loving messages to your partner while maintaining good boundaries.

You will probably be tempted to either not be loving or to give up on your boundaries too soon. Either one of these can undermine your attempts to help your partner. You must hang in there both with your boundaries, and with your love, and not give up on either of them until your relationship is over. That could be many years down the road or a few months later. It is the risk you take in taking action, but as I said before it is hardly as risky as doing nothing.

If you can, try to think about what your partner would need to be like if he or she were to help *you* to overcome a substance abuse problem. He or she would have to be tough enough not to give in to your abuse of the substance as well as loving enough to make you feel supported and loved. That is your aim. That is where you need to focus. Using the method of agreement can help you to express both your love and your boundaries without fighting. And, that's what this chapter is for.

Agreeing in the Midst of Problems

Let's consider a few example conflict areas to give you an idea about when and how to use agreement. The actual boundaries you use should be guided by your own counseling.

The initial confrontation

At some point after consulting with your counselor, you will need to address your concerns with your partner. If there is any danger in doing so, you will want to do this in a safe place and with other people present. Your counselor can guide you on that, also. For the purpose of my examples, I am going to assume that you have taken care of the safety issues.

Example use of agreement with a partner in denial:
YOU: "Matthew, I'm concerned about what's happening to our relationship."
SPOUSE: "(blaming) Well, if you wouldn't X, Y, or Z, then we wouldn't have problems."

> *YOU: "It's true, I'm doing things that are not helping our relationship. You're right. That's why I have decided to do something different."*
>
> *SPOUSE: "What do you mean?"*
>
> *YOU: "I'm learning how to help you with your alcohol problem. Because, I know if I don't, it will eventually destroy our relationship and you are too important to me to just let that happen."*
>
> *SPOUSE: "An alcohol problem? You're nuts, I don't have an alcohol problem."*
>
> *YOU: "Well, I could be wrong about it. But, until we can work on the problems in our relationship that seem to be connected to your drinking, I have to take care of myself."*
>
> *SPOUSE: "I don't need to convince you of anything. I drink, but I am in control of it. It doesn't cause any problems."*
>
> *YOU: "I have made a list of the problems I see and I have left it for you on your dresser. You don't need to read it, and you don't have to agree. And, it's your choice about how we move forward from here as a couple. I love you, so I hope you make a good choice for us. But, I won't fight you."*

(If you are dealing with a particularly tough partner, after this you may be staying with a friend, or someplace else. In your written letter explain this to your partner without giving your address. But, give your partner a way to contact you such as by email).

As you can see, this example comes from early in the process. It *is* confrontational, but it is not argumentative. You are presenting your view, but you are not insisting on anything. You even admit that you could be wrong. But, the problems still exist and need to be addressed. By leaving a letter, with the problems listed, at a different location, it gives your partner time to process it alone.

Your counselor may have you do the confrontation in a different way, but the main elements remain the same. Present your information, don't argue, express your love, and stick to your boundaries. I can't imagine any counselor suggesting to you that you argue with your partner. One thing to keep in mind is that although you may have made some decisions about your relationship and what you are willing to put up with and what you aren't, your partner has not yet had to face this decision. Give him or her the time and space to do that. Never require an instant answer when you present people with new information, or you will end up getting an emotional reaction rather than a well thought-out one.

Do be encouraged by the fact that every day many people are overcoming addictions. Those who have a strong and loving partner are the most likely to succeed. That's you! So, take care of yourself and be sure to stay in counseling until you don't need it anymore.

Dealing with his or her blame

One thing that substance abusers are very good at is blaming other people for their problems. As a spouse of a substance abuser, you are the most convenient person to blame. The blame can serve several purposes such as feeling more powerful, providing an excuse, and/or avoiding responsibility. But having reasons to blame you does not justify the behavior of blaming. And, it doesn't let your spouse off the hook for being responsible for his or her behavior. This is because no matter what you or anyone else has done, there are other choices your partner could make besides abusing drugs or alcohol. And when we have choices, we have responsibility for the choices we make.

Of course, you also have choices. Just because your spouse abuses drugs or alcohol, has run you into bankruptcy, has contributed to your child's anxiety or any of a dozen other things, doesn't mean the only thing you can do is sit back and blame your spouse.

You have the same choices as your spouse. You can blame, you can argue, you can avoid, you can divorce, you can help, and you can get help. No matter which of these choices you make, I can certainly understand your response. And, I won't judge you for it. But, if you care about your relationship and want to demonstrate what a loving person does when faced with a spouse who has a terrible problem, you will choose to help and to get help. You will not choose to be codependent—because that won't help either of you. You won't choose to continue to be a victim, because that won't help either. Helping always comes back to boundaries combined with loving messages. Let's consider an example of that.

Example of using agreement with a spouse who blames you for his or her substance abuse:

PARTNER: "If you took better care of those damned kids, I wouldn't be so stressed out that I needed to drink."

YOU: "Yes, I think you're right. Stress is part of the reason you drink."

PARTNER: "See? So, why don't you cut the stress out, then maybe I won't need to drink so much."

YOU: "I really wish I could just remove all your stress, but I can't."

PARTNER: "Then I guess I will just have to keep on drinking and it's all your fault."

YOU: "Well, you are right. I have let a lot of things just continue, and I'm working on changing that."

PARTNER: "You are, huh?"

YOU: "Yes, and it might mean needing to remove the kids from this environment. If

*that is what it takes to help you and them,
then I will do it."*
*PARTNER: "I didn't say you need to move
out."*
*YOU: "I know you didn't say it directly, but if
we are the cause of your drinking, then it
seems the only decent thing to do."*
PARTNER: "Well, they aren't that bad."
*YOU: "If you are going to use me or the kids
as your excuse for drinking, then you can
leave or we will. But, I'm not going to argue
with you about it or try to convince you that
we are not to blame. I can't convince you of
anything. All I can do is see what choice you
make and take the appropriate action. I
don't want to lose you, but if you are going
to reject me or the kids, then we will leave.
On the other hand, if you want me to help
you deal with stress in a better way, then I
will do that instead. You have the choice.
You have the power."*

By agreeing with your partner, you are actually letting your
partner dig his own hole. If he (or she) blames his job, then he can
get a different one. If he blames you, then he can leave or you can.
If the kids are to blame, then you can remove yourself and them.
You are not agreeing that you are to blame, but you are not
playing into the belief that your partner is a victim who needs to
abuse substances to cope. You are also not rejecting your partner,
blaming him, or wanting to leave. But you are showing him that
you are not afraid of that option. Love must be tough. And, I will
keep saying—work with your counselor as you do this.

Dealing with antisocial behaviors

One thing that often happens with people who abuse substances is that they cut themselves off from socializing with others. If they do socialize, it is likely to be with others who also abuse, or with people who have abused in the past. It is quite natural that someone who has a problem feels most comfortable being with other people who have the same problem. It isn't healthy, though. Being with others who also have substance abuse problems "normalizes" the substance abuse. That is, it doesn't *seem* like such a bad thing to do. But it is.

Being with others who used to abuse but who have stopped is healthy and a common part of substance abuse treatment programs. Early on, this may be a big step for your spouse—going from being with people who abuse substances to people who are in the process of quitting or have quit. But, as progress is being made, socializing with other people is also important. Should you argue if your spouse doesn't want to socialize with others? In my opinion, arguing drives more people back into substance abuse than it pulls out of it.

Better than arguing is to continue to give loving messages, while also continuing to use good boundaries. What this probably means in this case is that you continue to socialize with others, even if your partner does not want to or does not want you to. If that makes your partner upset, that is ok. Your partner doesn't have to, and certainly won't, like everything you do. Stop focusing on what your partner does or doesn't like. Start focusing on what is best for your long term happiness in the relationship. This means doing healthy things like having friends and a life. Following your spouse's idea of what's healthy wouldn't make sense because a substance abusing partner usually isn't the best judge of what the healthy thing is.

Example of agreeing with your partner when he or she refuses to socialize with your friends or family:
> YOU: *"My family has invited us over for a barbeque this weekend."*

PARTNER: "You really want me going to a barbeque where people are going to be drinking a lot of BEER?
YOU: "I already talked with mom and she said there's not going to be any beer. Just sodas and lemonade."
PARTNER: "Well they can drink whatever they want cause I don't want to be with that freak show family. We can have our own barbeque right here."
YOU: "Hey that sounds good. We can have a barbeque here, but I can't join you this weekend because I will be with my family."
PARTNER: "So, you would go, even if I don't? Do you really think that is being a good wife, a good partner? "
YOU: "That's right; I'm going even if you don't, although I wish you would."
PARTNER: "Didn't you hear me? I already said I don't want to be with that freak show."
YOU: "Yes, I heard you. "
PARTNER: "If you go, it means you care more about them than me. I don't know why I bother."
YOU: "You can think that if you want. I'm not going to argue about it."

Does this sound like an unproductive conversation to you? What has happened is that you have invited your partner; he or she has refused. You didn't argue, but stated your intention to go. Your partner tried to make you feel guilty. You didn't fall for it, didn't defend yourself, and refused to argue. This is very productive—provided that you follow up and go. Otherwise, you will lose respect big time. Losing respect makes it harder to help your partner. There is nothing to feel guilty about here because you are not doing anything that harms your partner. Your partner may harm himself by not going, but that is his or her doing—not yours.

Troubleshooting

Is everything going to just go smoothly when you do the right things? Hardly. People who use all the right techniques to climb Mt. Everest can still fall and break their leg. I don't tell you this to discourage you, but to encourage you. Because when you run into problems, you will see it as a normal part of progress rather than as a sign that you or your spouse has somehow failed. A person who goes off of his or her diet for a day has not failed and a substance abusing partner who relapses also has not failed. They have fallen—a step. What they need to do is get up again and start moving forward again. The same is true for you if you are working on agreeing, but find yourself arguing and fighting. You will have fallen, not failed. You just need to get up again and move forward again. Your spouse will have his or her own internal battle and you will have yours. But do you know that even the people who break their leg on Mr. Everest eventually make it to the top?

In this section, I try to anticipate some of the ways that you and/or your partner may fall (not "fail") in this process. You can also use problem solving to prepare for other problems.

"My spouse refuses to communicate or change."

You've heard it said that things "have to get worse before they get better," or that substance abusers have to "hit bottom" before they will work on making things better. This is often not the case, as most people will be willing to work on things when they are only moderately difficult. They don't have to go all the way to the bottom. And, for some people, all the way to the bottom includes suicide or prison, so we certainly don't want to intentionally drive people to the bottom.

The best thing you can do for your spouse is to take care of yourself. Make sure you are in counseling or coaching and learning how to use good boundaries. If you do this, then your spouse will gradually feel the weight of his own choices more and more and naturally become confronted with the possibility of losing you forever.

Hear me well, because I am *not* saying that you should threaten to leave your partner. I am saying to continue to express to your partner the desire to have a good relationship with him or her, but at the same time maintain healthy boundaries. Then, it won't be your decisions that results in your leaving your partner. It will be your spouse's decisions that make that happen—if it happens at all.

"Should I use agreement when my spouse is verbally or physically abusive or threatening?"

Definitely not. But, neither should you argue. Your safety and your children's safety come before any thought of intervention for substance abuse. That is because when violence occurs, not only can people be hurt or killed, but it also drives another spike into the heart of your relationship. Keeping yourself safe and your children safe are the best things you can do for your spouse. Your spouse doesn't need more things to feel guilty about.

Regarding verbal abuse, this is also not something to put up with. I recommend my clients to have a "zero tolerance policy" for verbal abuse. What this means is that the first time and every time thereafter that verbal abuse occurs they should immediately end the conversation without further comment, and preferably leave for an hour.

"Why zero tolerance for verbal abuse? Why not give a warning first?"

Would you respect someone who lets you abuse them once in a while or until you give a warning? I wouldn't. The other reason to have a zero tolerance policy is that your spouse will learn to self-monitor what he or she is about to say. If you use a warning system, then instead of learning to self-monitor, spouses will monitor for your warning. That means the abuse will continue to occur. If you want love, it is imperative that you earn respect. Allowing people to abuse you, even if it is just once in a while, will lower their respect for you, their love for you, and your ability to be a helpful partner.

"I'm too burned out to help my spouse."

You have gotten burned out as a result of either being patient too long, or using ineffective methods for too long. The result of either of these is for your feelings to shut down and your desire to continue your relationship to fall to practically zero. Perhaps the only thing at this point which keeps you in your relationship is putting off the hassle of getting out of it.

It's important to understand what is happening, so that you don't misinterpret your feelings. Your feelings shutting down is a natural way for your mind to get you to give up on expending emotional or physical energy which is not giving you any returns. It's a way of conserving energy. It is not a sign that your relationship is over or that you can never love your partner again. But, if you are to save your relationship and get your feelings of love back, you are going to have to change tactics. You are going to have to have some success, and that means using methods that are effective. As soon as you start to get positive results, your love for your spouse will start to come back.

Being burned out is also a sign that you need help because you just don't have the energy or motivation to learn new methods on your own. You will need some ways to recharge yourself without causing more conflict in your relationship. Entering counseling or getting marriage or relationship coaching at this time will help to give you the support you need as you start to make things better.

"I am afraid my spouse will choose the drugs or alcohol over me, and I will be rejected if I set good boundaries."

Unfortunately, this fear of rejection is what fuels codependency and is the reason that many relationships remain bad. In order to save your relationship, you have to risk losing it. But, in order to brave risking it, you must believe in yourself and have the resources to be able to live independently of your spouse, if necessary.

For example, a rich person wouldn't fear losing a job at a fast food restaurant, right? But, a poor person would be very afraid of that. So much so that she might let her boss abuse her. What if she learned how to survive and how to be able to get another job? Then, she could stand up to her boss to improve her working conditions. And, if her boss continued to mistreat her, she would leave. Her being able to improve her working conditions is similar to your being able to improve your relationship with your spouse.

You have to be able to survive without your spouse in order to be able to be strong and improve your relationship. Becoming less dependent (less needy) increases your value to your spouse while putting you at an equal level. It will also help you to focus on loving your spouse rather than on making sure that he or she loves and takes care of you.

Summary

Helping a partner to overcome a substance abuse problem is intimately connected to your ability to set healthy boundaries and take care of yourself. In fact, your partner may never seek recovery if you don't learn to have good boundaries and to take care of yourself. Simply attempting to take care of your partner without good boundaries is likely to result in your becoming codependent, and as a result, prolong the problems. Not effectively dealing with the problem will eventually lead to your burning out.

As with other problems it is not necessary to be mean to have good boundaries. In fact, arguing and hostility are counterproductive—they become excuses for your partner not to change and to focus on blaming you instead. If you remain loving, if you set and maintain good boundaries, and if you get guidance from a counselor, you have an excellent chance of helping your partner to overcome his or her addiction and to improve your relationship.

♥7♥

USING AGREEMENT TO RESCUE A RELATIONSHIP FROM SEPARATION OR BREAKUP

This chapter is not about agreeing that it is good for you to divorce or to breakup. It is about using agreement to start rebuilding a relationship with a partner who wants to divorce or break up. The method of agreement creates an opportunity for an improved relationship at such times, while other methods just make things worse. Traditional methods of responding to breakup make you appear insecure and needy while agreement keeps you in control.

Traditional Responses to Breakup

Traditionally (who started this tradition?), when one partner wants to break up and the other doesn't, an argument ensues. The person who wants to break up unloads all of the reasons why the relationship is no good. The person who doesn't want to break up then either apologizes and promises to do better, attempts to defend his or her behaviors, or cries and becomes quiet. If these don't change the mind of the person who wants to break up, raging or uncontrollable sobbing may follow. Each of these actions has predictable results and none of them help to rebuild the relationship.

Apologies and promises

The problem with apologies and promises is that they come too late. If the apologizing and promises had happened sooner, then they would have had more weight. At that time, the partner would still have been deciding about whether to end the relationship or not, and the apologies and promises would have acted to delay that decision. If the apologies were followed up with actual changes, the decision to end the relationship might never have been made.

When the apologies happen *after* the decision to end the relationship has already been made, the person breaking up sees the apologies as a desperate attempt to save the relationship rather than a sincere desire to change. So, no matter how sincere the apology may be at that point, it won't appear to be. Also, promises to change are not likely to be believed. After all, the partner who wants to keep the relationship already had plenty of opportunity to change. The fact that he or she didn't has led to the decision by the other partner that the change is not going to happen.

Defending and explaining

Defending and explaining, as you learned earlier, are part of the debate or argument method of persuasion. Since the result of arguing is always to make people more distant, this method of responding at breakup is even worse than making apologies and promises. At least the apologies and promises don't cause more distance.

When one person defends against the statements of the other, it becomes an issue of right and wrong. Either you are wrong and I am right (and I'm going to give you the reasons why), or you are right and I am wrong (which is totally unacceptable to me). There can be no win-win with a defensive reaction. The person who is ending the relationship is very unlikely to say, "I see what you mean. You had good reasons to do all those things that I hated. So, I guess that I don't want to divorce you after all." At least, I have never heard of this happening.

People don't make the decision to break up by reasoning. They make the decision to break up based on their feelings. They then use reasoning to support their decision. So, if you try to use reasoning to change your partner's mind, you will basically be saying that their emotional decision was wrong. It's as if you are saying, "Your feelings are wrong, so your actions are wrong, too. If you really understood me, then your feelings would be different and you would want to be with me." This message won't work. Just as you can't initiate a relationship with reasoning, you can't re-start a relationship with reasoning, either.

Crying and becoming quiet

Crying and being quiet can be an emotional reaction, a manipulative behavior, or both. As a purely emotional reaction, crying and becoming quiet are not bad at all. Crying gives an emotional release and being quiet prevents even more damage from being done by saying or doing harmful things.

When crying is used manipulatively, as a way to induce the other person to feel pity or sympathy, and so change their behavior, it *may* work. The time that it is most likely to work is if you rarely cry, your partner has a high degree of sympathy, and your partner feels somewhat responsible for the problems. At breakup, however, your partner's sympathy will be at an all-time low, your partner will have already come to the conclusion that his or her actions are necessary, and your partner will almost certainly have concluded that you are to blame. So, your crying is likely to be disregarded, or at best you will be soothed by a compassionate partner. However, your partner is still likely to break up with you.

Sometimes, when people fail to get their partner to change his or her mind about breaking up, they resort to prolonged and extreme crying. Again, this can be sincere or manipulative. The objective is to delay the breakup. If the partner who is breaking up is emotionally moved, he or she may attempt to sooth and calm the extremely sad partner. In the process of soothing, there may be some talking, apologizing, and defending that is actually productive, though it is a gut wrenching experience.

If the decision to breakup is delayed but the problems continue, the crying is not as likely to be effective the next time. Also, if the partner has often cried during the relationship, it is much less likely to get a sympathetic reaction at the time of breakup.

Loss of Respect

All three of these traditional methods (arguing, apologizing, and crying), whether they have some success or not, will result in a loss of respect for the partner who wants to save the relationship. If the person wanting to breakup gives in, he or she will lose respect. Either way, the loss of respect further erodes the relationship. I have worked with many people who have been rejected after using one of these three methods of responding. Without exception, we always need to work on regaining respect. Otherwise, they won't have a chance of successfully making up with their separated spouse or partner.

Pleading, arguing, and giving sex are certainly not going to work to rescue the relationship, though these are often tried. Women often forget that sex does not lead to emotional commitment for men. If you have *already* broken up or separated, I advise you to use the services of a relationship coach or counselor who specializes in reconciliation if you want to rescue your relationship. A counselor or coach who does not specialize in reconciliation will encourage you to let your partner go and move on with your life. The choice is yours.

Disconnection, Not Breakup, Is the Problem

It's interesting that people get so upset when their partner says they want to breakup or divorce. I say that "it's interesting," because in most of these relationships the couple have been emotionally disconnected for a long time. Surprise breakups do happen and it is understandable that they would be shocking— much like seeing a pet get run down by a car. Whether a surprise breakup or not, the main problem is not a partner's decision to break up. People can change their mind one way as well as the other. The main problem is the *emotional disconnection* on the part of the person who is breaking up. Instead of working to change the separated partner's mind, we have to work to emotionally reconnect.

People don't breakup when they are emotionally connected. That would be as difficult as disconnecting from an arm or a leg. Before the breakup, people who are contemplating breaking up gradually (usually) or quickly (sometimes) emotionally disconnect from their partner. Although they may continue to be sexually intimate, their role becomes more and more an acting job as they emotionally disconnect. Their loving behavior becomes internally "forced." This accounts for some of the surprise that men experience when their wives leave them. Because they have already emotionally disconnected, at the time of breakup they don't experience shock and their grief is minimal. They may or may not experience guilt, depending on how much they blame their partner for the need to break up.

If the partner who does not wish the breakup focuses on changing the mind of the person breaking up, he or she will create greater emotional distance—the very opposite of what is needed to rescue the relationship. A much more productive place to focus than changing the separating partner's mind is on emotionally reconnecting. Both connecting and reconnecting are two of the main purposes for using the method of agreement.

If a couple can emotionally reconnect, the relationship can be rebuilt, although it will take time. In my experience, although people often feel like breakup or separation requires immediate and desperate action, it doesn't. It can often be the start of reconnecting emotionally—something that has been needed for a long time. The "crisis" of breakup or separation is actually an opportunity for reclaiming the emotional connection that was lost. And that will take time. People who rush to stop the separation and treat it like an emergency are more likely to fail at reconciling than people who use a step by step approach. Relationships are *gradually* built or rebuilt. That can't happen in a day or a week. Attempting to repair a relationship suddenly is like trying to grow tomatoes from seed in a single day. The attempt to do so often just serves to convince both partners that the relationship is really over. Dramatic behavior makes for good movies, but in reality doesn't work very well.

Use Agreement to Reconnect

The agreement method is excellent for emotionally reconnecting and that is what is most needed if your partner is ending, or talking about ending, your relationship. What's more, unless your partner will have no communication with you, the reconnect is under your control. It is hardly possible for your partner to disconnect from you when you are in agreement. *Only disagreement disconnects.*

For your partner to disagree with you while you are agreeing with him or her, he or she would have to contradict himself or herself. That is, if you agree with your partner, your partner will have no choice but to agree with you. That creates connection. The connection or reconnection therefore, is under *your* control and only depends on how well you use the method of agreement.

What you have to be careful of during this process is not to slip into disagreement. Especially when your partner is first breaking up, the connections you make by agreement will be very weak. They are like a bridge built across a chasm using thread rather than rope. A single disagreement can be enough to break the thread—collapsing the bridge you have so carefully built with agreement. At this stage of rebuilding, I often help clients to respond to every message and communication from their partner. Later, as more connections are made, the bridge will become stronger and occasional mistakes won't break it.

Unlike most of the other times you use agreement, I don't recommend that you try to get to problem solving until after your partner starts to *desire* to rebuild your relationship. That could be soon after the breakup, if the decision was lightly made, but is more likely to come a few months after your separation if it was a well thought out decision. What do you do until then? You continue to strengthen the bridge. The bridge—the emotional connection between the two of you—is what all relationships are really made of. In a way, rebuilding a relationship from the point of breakup is like starting over. The major difference is that you are already aware of the areas of disagreement between you and your partner.

In a healthy relationship, people gradually build a strong emotional bridge, then become more committed to the relationship. Problems sometimes occur and are worked out as they happen so that they don't pile up and become heavy enough to collapse the emotional bridge. But, when someone breaks up, the problems have usually become too heavy—at least for the person who wants to break up. For them, the emotional bridge has collapsed and they are left standing on their own side of a deep chasm. The problems have gone beyond their ability to deal with and can't even be discussed. They see no way to repair the damage, to rebuild the bridge, and to feel in love again. They may even say at this time, "I don't love you anymore and I never will be able to again."

Working on problem issues is important, but when it happens, the relationship will have to be strong enough to deal with all the hard emotions that will come along with it. There is no such thing as simply rationally working out problems in a relationship. Even when we suppress our emotions, they still affect the outcome. If you are in a hurry to make up, you are likely to make the mistake of rushing to work out the problems. Even though the problems may have caused the breakup, they need to be put on hold. Working on problems with someone who doesn't care much whether he or she is with you or not is not likely to work out the way you want it to.

Why People Breakup or Divorce

There are many ways that breakup can happen, but the basic elements are the same. Your partner will either tell you he or she is ending the relationship because things aren't working, or because he or she has found someone else. While these seem different on the surface, actually they are pretty much the same message. People don't breakup simply because things aren't working. They only breakup when they have the hope of having something better. This bears repeating—people don't break up because of problems; they break up because of their hope of having something better.

A person with no hope of having anything better will not seek to breakup. After all, why go through the hassle of breakup if things are going to be just as bad afterward? So, whether partners have found someone else or not, their hope is that there is a better relationship waiting for them or that they can be happier on their own. And, their belief is that the relationship they have is never going to be as good as what they could have by breaking up or divorcing.

Most of the time they are wrong and the next relationship becomes just as bad or worse than the one they had with you. Although you won't be able to convince your partner of that at the time of breakup, hopefully it will make you less worried about your partner finding someone else. Still, you will need to work on changing some things about yourself to increase the chances that your relationship is going to be better than the next one he or she can find. If you are not the better choice, then your partner's decision to end your relationship makes sense.

If you have exceptionally bad problems like insecurity and/or abusiveness, that will have to change permanently before you can hope to win your partner back. If you can objectively see that you truly are a bad match for your partner, and you are unable or unwilling to change, then the most loving thing is to let him or her go. There is no shame in that. The shame would be if you want him or her back even though you know you would make him or her more miserable than someone else would. That is plain selfishness—not love. Although you may think that your desire to have your partner back is a measure of your love, a better measure is how much you care about his or her happiness. Love is not jealous and it is not selfish (1Corinthians 13: 4-5).

Agreement is the Best Response

To use the method of agreement, you need to be able to not have one of those three reactions listed at the beginning of this chapter (apologizing, arguing, or out of control crying). One of the most helpful things to do right away is to get space to "think things over." This is an excellent time to get support from your friends as well as enter relationship coaching. Remember however, that a professional coach will not help you to save a relationship quickly because that is not possible. But, a coach can help you to not do more damage when things are already bad enough, as well as set the stage for reconciliation.

Use Agreement to End Typical Breakups

Assuming that you have taken some time to calm down, it may be helpful to communicate mainly by email if you are in danger of losing control of yourself. Don't write a bunch of emails, though, and don't rush to respond to one. Having a well thought out answer is much more important than having a quick answer. In the next example, I will consider an email correspondence that has occurred after a breakup.

Example agreement email following a breakup:
Your Email: "I've thought about what you said. Although I am sad, there are a lot of things about your decision that make sense. Our relationship really hasn't been going well and just letting time go by is not making it any better."

Partner's Email: "I'm glad that you understand. We don't need to keep hurting each other. Breaking up is really better for both of us."

Your Email: "I wasn't quite ready for it, but maybe this will create some opportunities for us to be happier people."

There are many ways this could go, but what I want to show you in this example is that it is not necessary to agree that breaking up or divorcing is a good idea (in the example above, you never agree with the breakup). The basic agreement is that the relationship had serious problems and that now you both have new opportunities for the future. This matches the hope of your partner and also relieves your partner from feelings of guilt.

Although you might think that it is better for your partner to feel guilty, guilt distances people. It does not motivate people. Consider for example the number of Christians who have felt guilty about not attending church. Rather than it making them attend church more, it makes them put church more out of their minds and to downplay the importance of church attendance. People don't want to be reminded of what makes them feel guilty. Trying to "guilt" your partner into taking you back is like trying to attract a beautiful woman with a pair of smelly socks.

Use Agreement to End Hostile Breakups

Many times, people who are breaking up think they need to be angry and to have a dozen reasons ready to hammer their partner with at the time of breakup. This is the typical shouting and slamming doors kind of breakup. By provoking a fight, they feel better about leaving. The person who is left behind feels frustrated, angry, hurt, and betrayed. The best way to deal with this kind of breakup is to use the agreement method and under no circumstances defend yourself. Provoking a fight is just what your partner wants. But, that would just do more damage to your relationship.

Example use of agreement with a hostile breakup:
PARTNER: "I'm sick and tired of your jealousy and control and I'm not going to take it anymore. This is the end. I'm leaving you and you can find someone else to control."
YOU: "Well...I really can't blame you. No one wants to feel controlled."
PARTNER: "I have been telling you to knock it off for the past 2 years and you haven't

improved a bit. I don't know how your ex
could stand you as long as he did. But, now I
know why he left."
YOU: *"I sure haven't done well at*
relationships—either with my ex or with
you."
PARTNER: *"Well then, it shouldn't be hard*
for you to understand why I am out of here."
YOU: *"You're right—it's not hard to*
understand. Things have been very difficult
for you for a couple of years and you want
things to be better for you."
PARTNER: *"That's right."*
YOU: *"How can I help?"*
PARTNER: *"I don't know. Just keep away*
from me."
YOU: *"Ok."*

Again, you are not agreeing with the breakup. You are also not agreeing that you are the cause of the relationship problems. But, you are not arguing the point, either. In fact, you are not resisting your partner. He wants resistance; you don't give it. It's really hard for him to keep shouting if you don't oppose him. He won't be prepared for you to ask how you can help. He won't have considered that you would help. (I used a male in the example, but this is true for both genders). Although he says "keep away from me," don't take that as permanent. Nothing people say when they break up (or when they get married) is necessarily permanent—no matter how much they intend it at the time. Love and hate must be doled out day by day—there is no way to stockpile them for the future.

Being understanding works a whole lot better for reconnecting than convincing. Convincing is attempting to motivate someone to do something that you want. Understanding is what people desire, so the result is that they desire you more. Learn from the pros—listen and understand first. Guide later.

Use Agreement to End Replacement Breakups

This has got to be one of the toughest ways to break up. Not only are you being told that your partner doesn't want you any more, he or she has already replaced you with someone else. This means that your partner has been seeing someone else for a while. That behavior, which we can call cheating or adultery, depending on whether you are married or not, undermines the relationship and deals a severe blow.

I am not suggesting that you should try to save a relationship under this condition. You have every right not to. But, I want you to know that it is still possible. Elsewhere in this book, I deal with the topic of unfaithfulness, so here I will concern myself with the breakup that can accompany it. Breakup is not an inevitable result of unfaithfulness. Early on, unfaithfulness is a symptom of severe marriage or relationship problems. The longer it goes on, however, the more likely it is to lead to breakup or divorce.

Example use of agreement when your partner is leaving you for another:

> PARTNER: (Sends you an email saying that he or she has found someone else and is leaving you).
>
> YOU: (Take time for yourself to decide whether you still want the relationship. This will guide the way you respond to your partner. For this example, you have decided you will still try to save your relationship).
>
> YOU: (In a return email—easier; or face to face—much harder) "I must say that I was shocked to find out that you already have someone else and have decided to leave me. But, I'm not going to try to talk you out of it.

110

I really don't think fighting about it would be helpful, either. Because I still love you, what I want is what is best for you. If that means your leaving and being with someone else, then I won't stand in your way. I only hope that we can put our differences behind us and be friends."

Are you concerned this is agreeing with the breakup? While you are right that it is not opposing it (because that would cause further division and distance in the relationship), it is expressing love and concern for one's partner. Admittedly a very difficult thing to do after receiving such a rejection, but one which holds the most promise for reconnecting. At the least, it should give your partner some relief and perhaps may even provoke an apology. Remember however, you can neither guilt your partner back into the relationship, nor punish your partner back into the relationship.

If you are worried that your partner is continuing a relationship with someone else, you need to keep in mind that you have no power to break up that relationship. If you had such power, your partner would not have already decided to leave you. If you insist your partner dump his or her new relationship and stay with you, you are missing the point—*he or she is already gone.* Reconnecting (otherwise known as getting him or her to come back) at this point is much like dating someone who is also dating others, which is the way relationships typically are early on, before reaching the commitment stage. Your partner is not committed to you and may or may not be committed to his or her new partner. Your problem is *not* the other person. Your problems are rebuilding a positive connection and forcing yourself to go slowly.

There are other advantages to this approach. It may help you and your partner to be more honest with each other about many things that you would have fought about if you were still together. Also, if the reconnection is obviously not happening despite relating positively, it will help you to emotionally detach and to move on without having to tear yourself away. Your heart will not be broken as badly as with a bad breakup. I think that if partners can no longer love each other, at least they can minimize the damage. I've never known revenge or hatred to help anyone. The Bible says "Don't return evil for evil," (I Peter 3:9) and although there have been times I have felt like doing that, I end up feeling better about myself by being the bigger person.

Troubleshooting

"I already had one of those three reactions you say not to do. Have I blown my chances for saving the relationship?"

While you have done more damage to it, increasing the distance, you probably have not "blown it." As long as your partner and you still have contact and can communicate, you can start to rebuild a bridge between the two of you. I regularly work with people in this situation and most of them are able to make a positive connection, although some of them will not be getting back together with their partners. What I find is that people are still grateful for being able to recreate that positive connection, as it makes the divorce process easier, makes cooperating about the children and selling the house easier, and also makes it possible for them to remain friends. Understandably, some people don't want to be friends, but at least it is important not to be enemies.

"My partner was hostile to me, after I lovingly supported his or her decision to leave me for someone else."

If your partner has a hostile response to your loving support, your chances of getting back together are very slim. And, either you missed some severe problems in your relationship, or failed to do anything about them. If you still want your partner back under such conditions, it may be that you "need" your partner rather than love your partner. That, too, probably contributed to your relationship problems. If you desire a hostile partner who has already left you for someone else, then I recommend counseling for yourself. There is some big piece to the puzzle that you are missing and the counselor may help you to find out what it is. Even if you can't have your partner back, counseling may be very important for the success of your next relationship, as well as helping you to get over your current rejection.

"I am very upset and can't do any of this."

That's very understandable. My best advice is to take time to take care of yourself until you have some kind of peace of mind. Spend time with your friends, take support or comfort from any religious practices you have, and get counseling if things are feeling out of control or if you are having any thoughts of hurting yourself. If you don't take care of yourself, you will be giving evidence that your partner may be at least partially right about you not being a suitable partner. The best partners take care of themselves and are loving, but not needy. This is just as true after breakup as before. Although breakups feel like emergency situations, they are not. There is time. The most important thing is not to do more damage to yourself or the relationship.

"My partner cheated on me. Why should I be loving?"

You have a right not to be. You also have the right to try to keep your partner and rebuild your relationship. But, you can't do both. You will have to choose whether you will love or whether you will lose your partner. It is a value decision that only you can make. I help people who make the choice of love, but I understand the decision of those who don't.

Summary

Your partner breaking up or separating from you does not need to be the end of your relationship. If managed well, you may be able to rebuild your relationship. Working on emotional connection, rather than focusing on trying to stop the breakup, gives you the best chance of saving your relationship. Breakups are almost always a well thought out emotional and rational decision. Reasoning, arguing, pleading, and apologizing are not going to persuade a partner to change his or her mind. The only thing that can do that is if your partner once again desires to be with you. Not until then will he or she have the motivation to work on the problems that led to the breakup. You need to be the one to create that desire, through connection, as time alone won't do that.

Your first move should be to calm yourself, then use the method of agreement to build an emotional connection. Think of yourself as being in the early stages of dating your partner again— not as continuing a committed relationship. If you are disconnecting faster than you are reconnecting, then either you need to let the relationship go or you need to get professional help. The decision about whether to connect or disconnect is yours, but you cannot do both or something in the middle. That just wouldn't work.

♥8♥

USING AGREEMENT TO RESCUE A RELATIONSHIP FROM AN AFFAIR OR CHEATING

The method of agreement is an important part of the total intervention when your spouse has an affair. This chapter will also introduce you to important other steps such as the initial confrontation and good use of boundaries. Too many people become focused on ending their spouse's affair without considering they will also need to rebuild their relationship. So, they often do additional and unnecessary damage to their relationship in their initial steps. Interventions need to be effective; they don't need to be damaging. A successful intervention means ending the affair while maintaining an emotional connection to your spouse.

Unfaithfulness can only happen in committed relationships. A marriage is a committed relationship, as is an unmarried relationship where there is an *agreement* of commitment. If you are single, it's important to understand this. Some single people believe they are in a committed relationship simply by virtue of the fact that they are regularly dating someone. One of the most common mistakes that people make in pre-marriage dating is committing too soon and assuming that their boyfriend or girlfriend has committed to them as well. While some people only date one person at a time, others do not. Dating others is not cheating unless there is already an agreement of commitment in place.

It is not necessary that someone have sex in order for their behavior to be considered an affair. In marriage and other committed relationships, there are two kinds of affairs that can occur. One is called *sexual infidelity* and the other is called *emotional infidelity*. Let me define these for you so you can understand where I am applying the agreement method.

Sexual Infidelity

Sexual infidelity means that your spouse or committed partner is: 1) participating in some kind of sexual behavior with someone other than you, and 2) that behavior conflicts with an agreed on or understood expectation that you both have about the relationship. In order to be considered sexual infidelity, both of these things must be true. So, for example, in a culture or religion where it is acceptable to have more than one wife it is possible to be committed to one person, and have sex with another committed person, without it being considered sexual infidelity.

Although everyone draws the line differently on what is unfaithfulness, the above definition is the one used by marriage and family therapists in the United States. It does not include such things as visiting a topless bar, strip club, viewing pornography, or lustful gazes at people at a shopping mall. I won't include those behaviors in this chapter under unfaithfulness, although it could be argued that they are unfaithful as well. But, if we start going in that direction, we would have to say that misspending money and overeating are also kinds of unfaithfulness, or even lying about anything. If we start doing that, our definition of what is an affair will have no meaning.

You can see how in a new relationship, an assumption of commitment can cause misunderstanding about what is acceptable. Although women often make the assumption of commitment, sometimes it is men. Some men, for example, believe that if a woman has had sex with him, it means she has committed to him. In modern America, this assumption is dangerous for both men and women. It highlights the need for people to stop assuming and to start communicating clearly. When physical taboos disappear, verbal taboos need to disappear as well.

In addition, what constitutes "sex" also differs from person to person and culture to culture. For some, kissing is sexual, while for others it is casual. For some oral "sex" is not sex. This has been true since Bill Clinton was president. If you are single and don't discuss these things with your partner, you run the risk that your partner may do something you consider sexual that he or she does not.

Emotional Infidelity

Emotional infidelity occurs when your spouse or significant other is: 1) sharing intimate thoughts and feelings with someone other than you, and 2) the sharing involves secrecy which conflicts with agreed on or understood expectations that you both have for the relationship. As with sexual infidelity, both of these conditions need to be true for there to be emotional infidelity.

Perhaps even more so than with sexual infidelity, the expectations regarding emotional faithfulness need to be clearly understood before committing to someone. It is not prudent to assume that any two people will draw the lines exactly the same on sharing intimate thoughts and feelings with others. People may agree clearly on what is sexual infidelity, but be in disagreement on what is emotional infidelity. Your faithfulness depends, in part, on your spouse's expectations (and vice versa).

Notice that the definition of emotional infidelity, like the sexual one, does not specify the gender of the third person. What this means is that if you are a woman sharing with another woman or a man sharing with another man, your behavior could still be considered to be emotional infidelity by your spouse. Once again, it is better to clarify the expectations between you and your spouse or fiancé before having this level of involvement with *anyone* else. This is also the definition of emotional infidelity used by marriage and family therapists in the United States.

Traditional Approaches to Infidelity

Traditionally, one partner discovers the other to be having an affair after collecting evidence, or after catching their partner "in the act." The partner who discovers the affair reacts in a hostile or threatening manner and demands that the unfaithful partner get out. Either that, or the person who discovers the unfaithfulness leaves or breaks off the relationship. In a marriage, the person who discovered the affair may file for divorce at this time.

This kind of confrontation can have different kinds of outcomes. One possibility it that the person who is caught in the act or found out will beg forgiveness. This can then be followed with marriage counseling. This is a good outcome. Both partners will be on the same page in terms of wanting to get past the stress and conflict created by the adultery. Their presence in counseling will help them not only to address the unfaithfulness, but also to work on some of the issues that were present in the marriage prior to the unfaithful behavior. It is very unusual for there to have been no issues in the relationship prior to the adultery. The issues may have been hidden, but they were there.

Another possible outcome from the traditional confrontation is a total rejection of the offending partner. It is well within the rights of the person making the discovery. He or she will then soon be available to seek out a partner who will be more faithful. Although many people would applaud this as a good outcome, I only consider this to be a good outcome if that is what both partners really want. There are very many relationships, both married and unmarried, where unfaithfulness has occurred and subsequently led to the strengthening of the relationship after working through and rebuilding. I would encourage anyone contemplating leaving to at least explore first the reasons for the affair, and if there is still a basis for love and commitment, to work through it.

It is also possible that upon confrontation the unfaithful partner will want to end the relationship. If this occurs, it is not because of the confrontation. It could only be so if he or she were already preparing to leave and in fact, was close to actually doing just that. Your partner may have even not so accidentally let you

118

find out about the affair in the hope that you would break off the relationship. In this case, I would refer you to the chapter on breakups and separation.

There is yet another common outcome from the discovery of an affair, although it is not a confrontation. Some men and women will actually turn a blind eye to their partner's affair. There are many reasons for this, but it never creates a healthy situation. If you are such a person, I recommend you enter counseling and understand what makes your partner's behavior acceptable to you. If you complain about it, but do nothing about it, that is acceptance. The reason why people accept detestable behaviors is usually rooted in their own neediness and insecurity.

Before you confront your spouse

Decide on the *outcome* you would like to have before deciding how to confront your partner. If you are going to leave the relationship, then prepare to do that before confronting your partner. There may be many practical things to put in place first. I think this is a good first step regardless of what you would like the outcome to be, for a few reasons. First, if you are prepared at a practical level to separate from your partner, you will be able to have better boundaries when you do confront your partner; second, you do not know how your partner will react and should be prepared for the possibility of rejection; and third, it will force you to see the reality of what living without your partner will mean. You may feel very good having a strong emotional confrontation, but if you are then left with no place to stay and three kids to feed, you may find yourself wishing you used a different approach or prepared more first. This point is always overlooked by all the internet advice givers who simply say, "dump the bum," or "ditch the witch." Life is rarely as simple as that.

If You Want to End Your Relationship

If you decide you want out of the relationship and there are no children or properties to divide, you mainly need an exit plan. A confrontation is not even necessary. You can leave a note behind or send an email. The rest of this chapter won't be necessary for you either, as you will either avoid contact or fight. Fighting will cause even greater distance, assisting you in the breakup that you want to have. There won't be any reason to strain your brain cells coming up with good boundaries and methods of agreement.

On the other hand, if you still need to have cooperation from your partner after the breakup, such as with children or separating properties, I recommend you use the agreement approach. While it feels good to hurt someone who has hurt you, you will also be hurting yourself and any children by having a hostile breakup. Don't count on the courts to give you a fair deal. The courts idea of fairness and yours may be very different. And, cooperatively working with one lawyer can be much easier (and cheaper) than battling it out with two.

If You Want to Save Your Relationship

If you decide that despite all your anger, you love your partner, and you want things to work out if possible, then I recommend you read the rest of this chapter. You will have to do more than be confrontational and angry to save your relationship—even if your spouse is sorry for his or her behavior. You will need to start working on the processes of: 1) repentance (your partner stopping the unfaithful behavior), 2) forgiveness (moving beyond your desire for justice), and 3) restoration (which includes working on problems caused by the unfaithfulness as well as issues that were there before the unfaithfulness). Working with a professional such as a relationship coach or counselor is going to be helpful to manage some or all of these components.

But, even before you contact a professional, you will still have to have some communication with your partner. For that, I hope you find this chapter helpful.

The Confrontation

The confrontation is simply letting your partner know that the secret is out. It is not a discussion or negotiation. I recommend keeping this simple and short and also doing it in writing rather than face to face. Face to face may be gratifying, but it also has the potential for things to get out of control. When a bear is trapped in a corner, it will turn to fight, as will a mouse. Let your partner collect his or her thoughts and calm down before giving you his or her response, if any. Let me suggest to you a format for your note:

Example confrontation note:
"I have discovered ample evidence that you are having an affair. I am considering what I will do. I will listen to what you have to say, but if you deny the affair, either I will leave or you will have to. We cannot maintain a relationship with secrecy and lies."

Although you may want to talk about all of your feelings, blame your partner, or make threats, don't do it. Blaming or threats are never helpful, and this is not the time for talking about your feelings. There will come a time when talking about your feelings is very important. With this initial confrontation message, you are attempting to get your partner's attention, to get your partner to take you seriously, and to provoke an honest response. This note also contains the message that it may be possible to maintain your relationship, without stating whether you want to or not. That is very helpful for you, because this highly emotional time is not the best time for making such decisions.

Were you to give a message that you were definitely ending the relationship, when you would actually like to try to save it, you would create the following problems: 1) you would have to back down from saying that you are leaving, which would lose you more respect; 2) your partner might respond by rejecting you, putting you in a difficult position regarding reconnecting; and 3) you would be less likely to find out why your partner is having an affair. Don't assume you understand the reason for the affair. All you know at this point is that your partner is having an affair. The reason is very important to discover, even though it may be painful to hear.

Face to Face Confrontation

If you catch your partner in the act, then it would still be better to leave the scene, compose yourself, think out what outcome you want to have, and possibly consult with a professional before saying anything to your partner. Not much good is going to come out of a bedroom or back seat confrontation. And some words, even if hastily spoken, can never be taken back.

Avoid seeing your spouse as evil or as trying to hurt you

It is important to avoid seeing your spouse as evil. I recommend seeing your spouse much the same as if he or she had a drug or alcohol addiction. For sure, affairs and addictions are not the same thing, but usually serve a similar purpose. In some way, they help the person who is having an affair to temporarily feel better. Also, they both result in a loss of self respect, a loss of your respect, and damage to your relationship. Affairs, like addictions, are self-destructive as well as other-destructive. The affair may be the result of a character flaw (sometimes the case), and/or poor coping (often the case), and/or a symptom of an already failing relationship (usually the case).

Boundaries Come Before Agreement

You will need to use good boundaries as well as agreement in order to end the affair and stay connected with your partner. I would not ask you to agree with an affair any more than I would ask you to agree with drug or alcohol abuse. We can't agree with things that cause harm to our partners or our relationship.

Boundaries necessarily come first, because you must protect not only yourself, but also the relationship from further harm. That is the job of boundaries. Later will be time for seeking cooperation. For now, it will be in your best interest to force yourself to listen, to *think,* then to respond. Don't simply listen and respond. If you do that, you will either fight or be manipulated. Fighting will disconnect. Manipulation will lose you respect. Listen, *think,* and then respond.

Example initial talk following the confrontation:

PARTNER: "How did you find out?"

YOU: "Don't ask me how I found out. That's not the issue here."

PARTNER: "What are you going to do?"

YOU: "I haven't decided yet. I think it partly depends on you."

PARTNER: "What do mean? What do you want me to say?"

YOU: "I'm not wanting you to say anything. I am giving you a chance to say something. I will listen the best that I can. That's all I can offer you right now."

This message is consistent with my recommended confrontation (previous section). You maintain a serious, but non-committal tone and are still going for your partner's response. Hopefully, your partner will have an internal reaction of "I'd better lay out the truth here." Also, don't get pulled into providing proof of the affair. As long as you have sufficient proof for yourself, that is enough.

Example of listening to your partner's explanation/admission:

PARTNER: "I started talking to X about 6 months ago. I had no idea that we would get as involved as we did. I felt lonely and X made me feel special. I know what I did was terribly wrong. I don't blame you if you can't forgive me."

YOU: "Now, I can't forgive you, so don't ask me for that. I'm just listening and controlling myself. So, if you have more to say, you had better say it."

> *PARTNER: "As I said, it was wrong. It is*
> *wrong. I don't want to lose you. There is*
> *nothing I can say that can make it right, I*
> *know that."*
> *YOU: "Is there more you want to say?"*
> *PARTNER: "No, I think that's about it."*
> *YOU: "Ok, I will get back to you when I can."*

The point of this example is to show you how to listen to your partner without creating an argument. As long as you are focused on listening, there won't be an argument. Although you want to ask a lot of questions, this first time is not the time to do that. Now is the time to listen and think. Later will be the time to talk. Your partner will be very stressed, but don't worry about that.

Paving the Way for Marriage Coaching or Counseling

If you have confronted your spouse about the affair and all has gone well, your spouse will be willing to do almost anything to save your relationship. Although you could insist on marriage coaching or counseling at this time, which is not a bad idea, there is more you can do. You can help to increase your partner's *desire* to get coaching with you or to go to counseling with you.

If you can both get on the same page as far as what you want to accomplish in coaching or counseling *before* you get it, your sessions will be less stressful and more productive. After all, it is not the coach or counselor who will somehow fix your relationship. It is you and your partner working together which will fix your relationship. The coach or counselor can only guide. He can't do it for you.

Having been a marriage and family therapist for more than 15 years before becoming a marriage and relationship coach, I have seen all kinds of couples sitting on the sofa in my office. Some sat on opposite ends of the sofa with their arms crossed and looking away from each other. Others sat side by side holding hands. With no more information than this, you can probably guess which ones had an easier time of it in their first session, and also which ones were more likely to drop out before we had really started to get to work. If I can help you now to be in the position to begin coaching or counseling like the couples that were holding hands, my purpose will have been achieved in writing this book.

How do you get from the point of confrontation, hurt, and anger, to one of cooperation and hopefulness? How can we change the very bad thing that has happened in your relationship into an opportunity to have an even better relationship? For sure we can't do it with fighting. And we can't do it simply by forgiving and forgetting—which is impossible, anyhow. No, the only way that we are going to get there is by being able to agree on things that are really important and hold on to those as we move forward to deal with the really difficult stuff.

How to Rebuild with Agreement After an Affair

If your spouse has not yet stopped the affair, it is still not time for agreement. It is time for the continued use of your boundaries—perhaps on to the end of your relationship if your spouse doesn't soon stop the affair. After all, a spouse who refuses to stop an affair is more interested in saving his or her relationship with the other person than with you. Seeing the reality of that and taking care of yourself is important.

For the following examples, I am going to assume that after the confrontation and your proper use of boundaries, your partner has stopped the affair. Whether it is permanently stopped or not no one can know, but that is true for couples who have not experienced an affair as well. Our futures with our partners carry no guarantee against affairs, addictions, abuse, illness or death. We do the best we can for today to promote a better tomorrow. So try not to get too wrapped up in guarantees and promises. I certainly don't recommend that you ask for any. Just concentrate on working on today and the immediate future.

Example: No "forgive and forget"

PARTNER: "I have done what you wanted and I will never see her/him again. So, let's put this behind us and move forward. I want to have a good relationship with you."

YOU: "I want to have a good relationship with you, too. And, I want to be able to put this behind us and move forward, too."

PARTNER: "I'm relieved to hear that. Let's not talk about it again."

YOU: "I agree that we need to move forward, but we will need to talk about some things. Otherwise, we won't move forward. We will just end up where we were before this all happened."

PARTNER: "Yeah, so, what's wrong with that?"

YOU: "Well, where we were before was not good enough to keep you from having an affair. We need to strengthen our relationship so that it is less likely to happen again, and so that I can know you are really serious about moving forward with me."

PARTNER: "I told you it will never happen again. I just made a big mistake."

YOU: "Promises are not enough for me, now. If you want to continue to have a relationship with me, we need to work on things. That will also help me to forgive you, which I am not ready to do yet."

PARTNER: "I see. If you put it that way..."

It is too much to expect your partner to be eager to work on issues with you or to go to counseling unless you have set that as a condition of saving the marriage (an arm twisting maneuver). Whether pressured or not, your partner is going to imagine being repeatedly blamed for his or her behavior and would naturally like to just put everything behind him or her. That is neither realistic nor helpful.

Dealing with all your internal questions

Likely there are many things you want to ask your partner. If you are like most people, you will want to know how often they met, what they talked about, and what they did. If possible, I recommend you not go there. You are either likely to get the whole truth and wish you didn't hear it, or else hear more lies. The best time to actually talk about the details of what happened is later—after your relationship is going well again. It will be more useful, as some of the things that your partner was getting from the affair will be helpful for you both to include in your relationship together. Let the details go until later, if you can. For now, work on connection.

Example: A useful question

PARTNER: "So what do we do? How do we move forward? Are you saying we need to go to counseling or something?"

YOU: "Yes, I think that will be important, but not just yet. First, we can just work on understanding each other a little better."

PARTNER: "How do we do that?"

YOU: "Let's go for a walk or go out for a coffee. I have something to ask you, but don't worry. It's a positive thing."

PARTNER: "Alright..."

[While walking or at the restaurant]

YOU: "I don't want you to tell me why you had the affair. I want to ask you rather, why do you want to stay with me? When you are

> *done, I will tell you why I want to stay with*
> *you."*
> *PARTNER: "I love you. I mean I know I*
> *messed up and did something that makes it*
> *seem like I don't love you, but I do. You're*
> *my husband/wife, and I don't want to lose*
> *you..."*
> *YOU: "I am very hurt and angry, but I love*
> *you too..."*

Can you see the agreement building the connection here? If you were to instead ask about the details of the affair, it would be hard to get to this place. If it is your husband who had the affair, I recommend going for a walk when having this talk. Men talk better when they are active and not face to face. If it is your wife who had the affair, then I recommend the restaurant. Women talk better face to face while being mostly inactive.

Building a better relationship with agreement

Undoubtedly your partner will want to start rebuilding your relationship right away because he or she is eager to get away from talking about the actual details of the affair. I recommend that you don't make any promises to not talk about the affair. There is no reason to comfort or reassure your partner about this. Later, when forgiveness is possible, will come the time to stop talking about it. Before that, it's important to talk about for many reasons. One of the most important reasons to talk about the affair is to find out what your spouse was getting from the other man or woman that he or she was not getting from you.

This is not something you try to do right away. This comes in the rebuilding stage and preferably after you are working with a marriage coach or counselor. That can really help the information to be used to build up rather than to tear down. The following conversation is one that could happen in coaching, possibly in counseling, and maybe on your own if you are very secure and your emotions are under good control.

Example of using information about the affair in a positive way:

> YOU: *"I need to know what you got from your affair with X that you weren't getting from me."*
>
> PARTNER: *"I don't want to go there. It will just cause fighting and I think it would be going backwards. We agreed to work on making things better, not worse."*
>
> YOU: *"You are so right. I don't want to fight with you either. I'm not looking to blame you now and I am calm. What you did was wrong, but there was a part of you that was reaching out for something you really needed. Knowing what that was can help us to build that into our relationship."*
>
> PARTNER: *"But, that will sound like I'm complaining about you. You are fine. I am the one who messed up."*
>
> YOU: *"I agree that I'm not to blame for the affair. And I'm probably not to blame for not being aware of your needs, either. But, your needs are important. Please help me by talking about what was really good for you about your affair."*

Can you tell from reading this that this should not be something you do early on? It really can't be avoided at some point though, because the answer will point at something that was missing in your relationship. Whatever the answer is, it is something that needs to be dealt with. It is too unrealistic to believe that your partner is no longer going to have that need just because he or she is no longer having an affair. He or she might have that need more than ever now. Failing to deal with it could eventually lead to your partner being tempted to have another affair.

What to do with your spouse's answer

When your partner tells you what he or she got from the affair that he or she was not getting from you, there will be a temptation to either defend yourself as having provided that or to blame your partner for not having let you know. Although you might be right on both counts, it won't be useful to do that. Even if you believe you provided everything your partner ever needed, you must admit that your partner did not feel that way. Maybe he or she should have, but we can't deal effectively with what *should have been*. To make a better relationship, we need to focus on what can be. We have to pick and choose what we want to say even in a very open relationship.

Example of agreeing with information about the affair:

> PARTNER: "Well, he made me feel so cared for—like I was really important for him. I hadn't felt that way for a long time and it was hard to resist that. I guess I didn't resist that. I tried, though..."
>
> YOU: "Feeling cared for is really important for everybody."
>
> PARTNER: "Yeah. I didn't realize how much I needed that."
>
> YOU: "Right now, I want to talk about ways that I can help you to feel cared for. Maybe you can remember some things that he did, or can think of some other things that really help you to feel cared for. If I can, I want to help you feel that way again. If I can't, then that will be good to talk about, too."

In this example, you can see that a contrite partner has given openings for you to be able to jump in and blame her or hurt her. This happens not just because a person feels contrite, but often because a person will want to put out a little test before opening up. If you become blaming or critical, then they are not going to open up. If you remain focused on being loving and positive, as in this example, your partner is much more likely to open up.

In these examples, it seems quick and easy. That's because they are only snippets cut out of many hours of conversation and togetherness. It will take time and work for both of you—helping each other to feel comfortable enough to be open about what you are both thinking and feeling. It will also take time to be able to really listen. Many people can't do this on their own as their conversations break down into conflict. You will need to accurately gauge your ability to do this and the progress you are making. There is no reason that a relationship can't be better after an affair than before, but like building a house of cards, it requires careful attention and gentle moves.

Troubleshooting

Anticipating problems is an important part of dealing with them. Here, I try to anticipate some of yours.

"My partner is terrible. I am too upset to do any of this. Your approach seems too easy on the unfaithful partner and it is not fair."

I agree with you (are you surprised?). There is nothing fair about it. Something tragic and terrible was done to you and to your relationship. If you want out, I can't blame you and I wouldn't try to talk you out of it. But, if you want to save your relationship, focusing on fairness and justice won't help.

It's not all easy on your partner, though. When you use good boundaries, there will be some justice. Although it won't bother you, your partner will experience a loss of whatever he or she had with the other person. It must have been significant for him or her to risk his relationship with you.

If you are too upset, take care of yourself first. Get help from your friends or family, or from a counselor. You need to be able to have good boundaries and still be loving. If it takes time for you to be able to do that, or if you need to separate to be able to do that, then separate. Anything that will get in the way of you having good boundaries has to be dealt with first or none of this will work.

"My spouse has done this before. Is there something different that I should do, some modifications I need to make?"

It is really important that you have a professional helping you to figure out what is contributing to the repeat affairs. You need to know if it is a character issue or mainly a relationship issue. The more it is a character issue, the more important it will be for you to protect yourself and also consider divorce. The more it is a relationship issue, the more you will need help with changing what is going on in your relationship.

"I also had an affair that my spouse knows about. Does this make us even?"

It's quite cliché, but two wrongs don't make a right. It is a definite sign that although you both want to be together, you are both having a hard time getting your needs met with each other. Having had an affair yourself might make you more sensitive to some of the reasons your spouse has now had one. It doesn't change what you need to do, but it underscores your need for couple's coaching or counseling.

"I'm afraid that if I set good boundaries my partner will leave me."

If you don't set good boundaries, you also guarantee that your relationship won't last. Respect is earned by having good boundaries. The weaker your boundaries, the harder it is for your partner to respect you, and to love you. Most people would rather take a chance on their partner leaving than to guarantee a loveless or emotionally distant, unequal relationship.

"My spouse is demanding that I show the proof for his or her affair."

As long as you have proof, don't show it to him or her. Your spouse not knowing will help him or her to resist the temptation to have another affair. If your partner denies having an affair because it hasn't been proven, don't fall for that silly game. Just continue as though your partner is refusing to give up the affair.

"I'm undecided about whether to divorce or not."

That indicates your mixed feelings. It isn't something you have to figure out all at once. Better is to have a strategy for dealing with those feelings. I recommend putting all of your heart into the intervention I suggest—love, boundaries, professional help, and no fighting. The outcome of that process will help you to be more clear about whether to divorce or not.

Summary

An affair or even multiple affairs don't have to spell divorce or the end of your relationship. There are many couples who have gone through the pain of one or more affairs and been able to work through the issues to have a better relationship. How to do that is not intuitive or natural. Our feelings make us want to be too hard at times and too soft at others. It's important to have a plan and guidance. As with other problems, fighting will lead to more disconnection, so that isn't a good method for dealing with an affair. When dealing with an affair, it's important to put good boundaries into place and to require certain changes in behavior *before* working on connecting with agreement.

Most of us have an irrational belief that if we clearly explain situations to angry people, they'll realize they were wrong and we're right. This belief is nothing short of delusional.

Albert J Bernstein PhD
from *How to Deal with Emotionally Explosive People*

♥9♥

USING AGREEMENT TO PUT AN END TO BLAME

No one likes being blamed for anything, but some people are more sensitive to blame than others. It depends on our experience with blame in the past. It also depends on how secure we are in our relationship. If we are blamed by someone very close to us, it can either cut us like a knife, or it can be just like a pinprick, depending on what we believe the blame means. If we experience blame as rejection, it hurts a lot. If we experience it as correction, it doesn't hurt so much, but we still don't like it. Blaming someone is like throwing water on the fires of love. Blame too much and the fires of love go out. When we get blamed too much, we stop loving our partner. And, no matter how right we are, if we regularly blame our partner, our partner will stop loving us.

Blame can pile up. If our relationship with our partner is already not close, each time we are blamed it is mentally added to the pile of things we don't like about our relationship. Then when conflict erupts, we react to all the accumulated frustrations in our relationship. At that time, our partners will accuse us of overreacting, and of course they will be right. When a lot of gas has leaked into a room, even a tiny spark can set it off. So it is with accumulated blame and hurt.

What agreement can do for us is to change blame into something positive and useful. That prevents blaming from piling up. The method of agreement can make blame an occasion for building our relationship. In a positive way, it reduces how much we get blamed by others. You will no longer have to tell your partner to stop blaming you. When you use the method of agreement, your partner can no longer hurt you nor correct you with blame, and so the blaming will stop.

Characteristics of Partners Who Blame

If this chapter is of interest to you, it's likely that you are blamed a lot by your spouse. That is a different experience than occasionally being blamed by a loving and reasonable spouse who just happens to be right. With such a spouse, we fess up. Yes, indeed, what we said or did was inappropriate and we are sorry. We know in that case that we have unintentionally stepped on our spouse's toes and that probably there were many times when we could have been blamed, but because of his or her love for us, we got a pass. Love is patient, but sometimes does need to speak up for itself after all.

People who blame a lot usually resist looking at their own contribution to the problems. If you are blamed for being impatient, for example, your partner may not take any thought to why that might be so and how he or she may be contributing. You may be blamed for being sexually unresponsive but your spouse may never take a look at the way he or she treats you during sex and at other times, too. You may be blamed for being a bad parent by a spouse who never takes his or her turn at parenting.

People can also be blamed for the feelings of another. If a blamer feels bad, then he or she thinks that someone else must have done something to cause that feeling. If a blamer has abusive behavior, whether it's toward others (such as verbal or physical abuse) or towards himself or herself (such as with addictions and/or isolation), then he or she will believe someone else to be the cause—"It's my mother's fault," "It's my husband's fault," and so on. If a blamer is fired or rejected, then he or she blames the boss or employer. This characteristic of not seeing oneself as responsible largely explains why blamers don't try to change. They don't believe that anything is their fault, so they don't believe that their changing would help. If you feel stuck or like a victim, there is a good chance that you are a blamer, too.

As I wrote in my book, *What to Do When He Won't Change*, change cannot be initiated by a person who blames, because he or she believes that improvement can only result from other people improving. He thinks, "If she weren't so bad, then I wouldn't be so mad." Women also can be blamers, though they more often have the thought, "If he weren't so bad, then I wouldn't be so sad." Blamers have a great deal of self pity and a whole lot of anger toward others. After all, they perceive others as making them victims. In relationships, they feel that they have to put up with their partner's inadequacies and take care of him or her at the same time. Relationships don't feel fair to them. Their blame creates internal resentment, and their resentment prevents them from feeling any kind of long term deep love.

The end result of blame is self-harm, harm of others, rejection, and loneliness. A partner of a blamer has a chance to escape, but for a blamer, there is no escape. His or her hope lies in finding a perfect person, but such a person doesn't exist. *Everyone* will eventually fail them in some way, so everyone will be blamed for their continuing unhappiness. They feel perpetually frustrated.

If you have such a partner, then I encourage you to see how much he or she needs your help. As with many other things, if you can be both tough and loving, you can initiate the process of change that he or she cannot.

Typical Reactions to Blaming

What do you usually do when you are blamed for something? Do you become sympathetic and apologetic? Do you become angry and defensive? Do you become quiet and emotionally shut down? Do you become argumentative and attacking? Do you clarify what your partner is saying and work together with him or her to make your relationship better? If you do that last one, then you are in the minority and I will excuse you from reading this chapter. Doubtless there is very little blaming that happens in your relationship anymore.

If you do tend to become defensive or hostile, that's quite understandable. But, being understandable and being helpful are two different things. Being hostile or defensive won't do anything to change the blaming or improve your relationship. Being right won't make it right. What good will it do to be able to justify your emotional reactions if you and your spouse are becoming more and more distant? That will just lead you to the point where you feel justified in divorce.

Like the other problems in this book, blaming is characteristic of both a behavioral and an emotional problem. The way you respond to blaming will either encourage or discourage the continued use of blaming. Although our partners may experience a release of tension when they blame us for something, that tension builds again. As this pattern of tension build up and blame continues, they gradually lose us emotionally, if not physically also. The extent that we help them to change is the extent to which we help them to have a more fulfilling relationship with us.

Helping someone who blames is a gift of love and probably one you don't feel like giving. In the short term, it is much more satisfying to put the blamer in his or her place. But in the long term, it really isn't. The most satisfying thing in the long term is to create a close relationship, free from blame, that is good for both you and your spouse.

I also want to suggest to you that you do have some responsibility in the matter. As I say about abuse, anyone can make you a victim the first time. But, for us to continue to be a victim, we must continue to play the role of a victim. Had you established good boundaries the first time you were blamed by your spouse, and maintained them, it is very unlikely that your spouse would still be blaming you now. Don't get me wrong—you are not the cause of your partner's blaming. But, the way you respond enables your spouse to be able to continue to blame you.

In this chapter, I will help you to respond to blaming by using the method of agreement. Far from it making you contrite and powerless, you will gain both power and respect. The most valuable place to be, in a committed relationship, is at a level equal to your partner. You have to earn respect before someone will consider you to be an equal. Boundaries and the method of agreement will help you to earn that respect.

You will also find the method of agreement helpful in other venues where you experience blame. That might be with other family members, at work, or even with friends. Will these people still want to hang around you if you stop them from blaming you? It depends on the person. All I can say is that they will have more respect for you, and that will give you the opportunity to have a closer relationship with them. For you to continue to be submissive and bear the brunt of their blame just so they will remain your friends would cheat you (and them) out of the closeness you otherwise might have.

Distinguishing Blame from Verbal Abuse

I think it's important to be able to distinguish clearly between blame and verbal abuse. From my perspective as a marriage and relationship coach, it is important to make this distinction because the method for dealing with each of these behaviors is different. Blame can be managed with agreement, but agreement should never be used with abuse.

When someone is being verbally abused, I recommend the immediate use of a boundary such as walking away with no further communication—what I call a "zero tolerance policy" for abuse. With blame, however, it is more helpful to work on changing the communication rather than just stopping it. Walking away would be counterproductive because it wouldn't substitute anything in its place. Also, walking away may feed into the power your spouse feels when he or she blames you.

Verbal abuse can come in different forms and is somewhat subjective. Some of my clients draw the line differently than I do. Instead of getting them to change where they draw the line, we focus on what to do when their line is crossed. For me, verbal abuse happens when someone calls us a bad name (as opposed to a good name), compares us to something else which is bad, or otherwise disparages our character Here are examples of each:

A bad name:
"You are a bitch"
"You are a butt hole"
"You are stupid"

A bad comparison:
"You are like a vampire, sucking out my life blood and happiness"
"You are like my ex-wife"
"You are like a mentally retarded person"

Character assassination
"You are unlovable,"
"You are nothing but a @#$@ing liar"
"You don't care about anyone but yourself"

Wherever you draw the line between abuse and blaming, be sure that you live according to your standard on both the receiving and the giving end. You will lose a lot of respect if you either allow your partner to abuse you or if you abuse your partner. Losing respect is one of the fastest routes to losing your relationship.

There is no "half-way," with abuse. It makes no sense to say or think, "He (or she) *kind of* abuses me." Either it is abuse, or it isn't. Also, there is no "sometimes acceptable," with abuse. It is never accepted by healthy people. Saying "He only abused me *a little*," is as ridiculous as saying, "He only got me pregnant a little."

If you are the victim of verbal abuse, there is a lot you can do to stop the abuse and save your relationship (in that order). In severe cases, the verbal abuse can often be stopped in as little as two weeks. But, you won't find detailed information on that in this book because the method of agreement is *not appropriate* for the initial stages of dealing with an abusive partner.

The rest of this chapter will be concerned with blame which does not have any of the three characteristics of verbal abuse that I listed in this section.

What is Blame?

To be more effective at using the method of agreement with blaming, it will be helpful to take a look at just what blaming is. Blaming is when someone attributes the cause of an undesirable event to someone else, *whether or not* they are the actual cause. Take any bad event, and say someone is responsible for it, and you are blaming them. Whether you are right or wrong, you are blaming them.

What is the difference between blaming and complaining?

Blaming is directly attributing fault. Complaining is saying what we don't like, but without a direct attribution of fault. Let's look at some examples:

Blaming:
*"**Because of you**, we never have any fun."*
*"**It's your fault** we don't have any money in the bank."*
*"**If you didn't** hang out with your friends all the time, we would get along better."*

Complaining:
"I hate it that we don't have any fun in this relationship."
"I don't like the way all of our money goes to buying unnecessary things."
"I don't like you hanging around with your friends all the time."

For some people, these will sound like exactly the same thing. That is because they mentally add the attribution part. That is, although their partner didn't say it, they mentally add on to their partner's statement "because of me." Then they react to their partner's statement plus their own addition. They react as though they were blamed.

Example:

> *Partner 1 <u>Says</u>: "I hate it that we don't have any fun in this relationship."*
> *Partner 2 <u>Hears</u>: "Because of you we don't have any fun in this relationship."*

If you mentally add on to what your partner is saying, it allows your partner to be more effective at saying less while also being able to deny blaming you. So, in regard to the complaining example above, if you say, "So, it's my fault that we don't' have any fun?" your partner can easily reply, "I didn't say that."

If you don't mentally add the blame piece, your partner has to actually say the attribution in order to blame you. If you have a passive partner, it's particularly important to only take what he or she actually says, so as not to be codependent for the limited communication. That is, if you want your partner to talk more, you have to stop mind reading, even if your mind reading is 100% correct.

General Blaming Problem or Specific Area?

If you are being blamed in a specific area, such as your spouse's affair, substance abuse, parenting problems, or other, I recommend that you focus on dealing with those problems as outlined in other chapters. If the blame is more general or varied, then it reflects a communication style rather than a problem with any single area. In such case, you should find the method of agreement, as used in this chapter, to be helpful.

Why Do People Become Blamers?

As a marriage and relationship coach, I am more concerned about helping people deal with other people's blaming in an effective way than I am in figuring out why the other person is blaming. There is a common misconception that if you know the reason for a person's behavior, you will know how to change the behavior. This could not be further from the truth, whether the behavior is someone else's or your own. For this reason, psychology is moving away from insight oriented therapies ("aha, that's why I don't like spinach") in the direction of cognitive-behavioral therapies (how to think and behave differently).

I don't mean to say that insight oriented therapies are useless or that it's a waste of time to figure out why someone does something. A major value in understanding the origin of a problem is to go easier on ourselves and others. We are the way we are for a reason. Others are the way they are for a reason. People do not choose harmful personality traits intentionally. If your spouse frequently blames you, it is not because he or she has decided that blaming you is the best way to deal with your relationship. He or she simply does it because that way was somehow learned in the past and continues to be somewhat useful.

Why He or She Continues to Blame

If you really want to get at the "why" of what a person is doing, you need to take a look at the results of what they do. Because it is the results which maintain the behavior. They *learned* the behavior in the past, but they continue it because of the results in the present. Those results can be both internal and external.

Blame typically relieves an internal pressure such as guilt or perfectionism and/or an external one by creating distance in the relationship. The most likely reason that your spouse is blaming you then, is to either absolve himself or herself of responsibility (reducing guilt), correct you or fix you (relieving an internal perfectionism pressure), or create distance (maintaining a comfort zone or providing an excuse to do behavior that is harmful to your relationship).

My recommendation is that you don't get caught up in the "why." Instead focus on helping your spouse to find a less harmful way to accomplish what he or she normally accomplishes with blaming. There are better ways to get some space, and there are better ways to help people improve. There are also better ways to deal with guilt.

Blaming others is a short term strategy with negative long term consequences. Helping your spouse to shift to another method that is less destructive is a worthwhile goal for your relationship.

Stop Being Codependent for Blaming

The method of agreement, together with good boundaries and loving messages, creates new patterns of relating. Many of the boundaries for blaming relate to no longer responding in a way that makes the blaming successful. For example, if your spouse is blaming you for things that he or she feels some level of guilt about, and you accept responsibility for them, you are being codependent—you are helping your spouse to avoid responsibility by blaming you. A healthy boundary in this case would be for you to no longer take responsibility for something that you didn't cause.

If your spouse is seeking to "perfect" you or "correct" you through blaming, then accepting such correction would be codependent. A healthy boundary would be to no longer accept correction *in this way*. Although your spouse may be right about your need to change, accepting the blaming would be a codependent behavior helping to maintain your partner's blaming.

Your spouse may be using blaming to maintain distance that supports his or her harmful relationship behaviors. If so, then boundaries which end those behaviors also would take away the rewards of blaming. This use of blaming reminds me of elementary school children trying to escape punishment by blaming someone else for "starting it." The fact is, it doesn't matter who started it—if a behavior is wrong, it is wrong. Never hold yourself accountable for your spouse's problem behaviors.

Putting boundaries into place will make the method of agreement more effective. Without boundaries, you will be rewarding your spouse's blaming at the same time you are trying to shift him or her from a blaming style to a cooperative one. The net result will be frustration for you. You will give up and say that agreement doesn't work. It would be like trying to drive a car without fuel. That would be frustrating and you might conclude that your car doesn't work. But you wouldn't do that, because you know better, right? Cars need fuel whether it's gasoline, diesel, ethanol, or electricity. Likewise good communication, which you will use to build your relationship, cannot be effective without your having good boundaries. These two things go together—boundaries and good communication. Either one alone will not get you to where you want to go.

Stopping Your Own Use of Blaming

What would happen if you tried to stop your spouse from blaming you, while you continued to blame your spouse? Not only would you not be effective, but you would lose respect. You can't hold your spouse to a standard you don't keep for yourself. You would come off as a hypocrite and any boundaries would seem terribly unfair to your spouse.

If you currently blame your spouse for anything, ask yourself if blaming is really helping. You must start there because as long as you think it helps a little, you will continue to do it. Partial success maintains your spouse's behaviors, and it will maintain your behavior, too. If you do think your blaming helps a little, make a list of all the costs and benefits you get from blaming your spouse (whether he or she deserves it or not). That too, should help you to let go of blaming.

Finally, if you are blaming and want to stop, you need to substitute some other behavior whenever you have the urge to blame. In general, we should never blame or complain about anything, unless we are prepared to take *action* to do something about it. If you must blame or complain, then obligate yourself to do something about it. For example, if you complain that your taxes are too high, then write a letter to the government, support a candidate who promises to lower your taxes, or any other appropriate action. If you are unwilling to do that, then don't complain. It will just make you feel worse without making the situation any better.

Likewise, if you complain about your spouse, or blame your spouse for anything, take responsibility for doing something about it. If there is nothing you can do, or you are unwilling to do anything, then accept it and work around it. Blaming and complaining, without action, will only make you feel like a victim, make you less attracted to your spouse, and also make your spouse less attracted to you.

After you have stopped blaming and complaining for *three months*, then work on helping your spouse to change. Why three months? Because that will make sure that you are not just suppressing your blaming, but have really changed. Every time you catch yourself blaming, reset your count to day zero. Work at it until you get to three months without blaming.

Using Agreement to End the Blame

Using agreement with blame is a little different from using agreement with other behaviors. Generally, agreement is not used with the problem behavior itself. For example, you wouldn't agree that it is good for your partner to abuse alcohol or have an affair, but you might agree that there are stresses and problems in the relationship that need to be dealt with somehow. In the case of blame, your partner is unlikely to see blaming as a good thing. In fact, your partner is likely to not like to "have to" blame you. Because of this, you and your partner have something in common. You don't want your partner to "have to" blame you either.

Example of how blaming might typically go:
SPOUSE: "It's your fault that my friends don't visit anymore. You're always so rude they can't stand to be around you, and I don't blame them."
YOU: "I'm not rude. I just leave the area so I don't have to listen to their dumb talk."

Explaining your behavior is a defensive reaction. While it may be accurate, it isn't helpful. Your partner is not likely to think, "Oh, he's (or she's) right, my friends do talk about dumb things, so it's probably better if he (or she) clears out when they come over." Such a response would require your partner losing so that you could win. Arguing about whether the friends' talk is dumb or you are rude is likely to bring in other examples of your "rudeness" and the friends' "dumbness," without anything being resolved.

Example: Use of agreement when you are actually not at fault

> SPOUSE: "It's your fault that my friends don't visit anymore. You always are so rude they can't stand to be around you, and I don't blame them."
>
> YOU: "It's true. I do leave the area when they come over."
>
> SPOUSE: "Right? So, because of you, I can't have any friends."
>
> YOU: "It really does seem like it's hard for you to keep friends."
>
> SPOUSE: [becomes silent]
>
> YOU: "Look, let's talk about some ways that I can help you to have more contact with friends."
>
> SPOUSE: "Ok, but I can tell you the solution right now—just don't be rude to them when they come over."
>
> YOU: "Ok, we can start with that. You might be right. It might be a really good idea. Let's take a look at that and some other ideas, too. [You take out a piece of paper and begin problem solving with your spouse]."

What I want you to see in this example is that your partner's blaming creates an opportunity for arguing, but it also creates an opportunity for closeness, through the method of problem solving. Which way it goes is really under your control. If you want to take it to problem solving, then use the method of agreement with each blaming statement your partner makes. Then shift to problem solving as a way to help your partner with something he or she wants. It's not a deception. You will be helping your partner as well as yourself.

Perhaps you are thinking that agreement might work if your partner goes along with the problem solving, but if he or she doesn't, then you are in just as bad of a situation as before. Let's take a look at that.

Example: Agreement when your partner refuses problem solving

> SPOUSE: "It's your fault that my friends don't visit anymore. You always are so rude they can't stand to be around you, and I don't blame them."
>
> YOU: "It's true. I do leave the area when they come over."
>
> SPOUSE: "Right? So, because of you, I can't have any friends."
>
> YOU: "It really does seem like it's hard for you to keep friends."
>
> SPOUSE: [becomes silent]
>
> YOU: "Look, let's talk about some ways that I can help you to have more contact with friends."
>
> SPOUSE: "No, I'm not going to talk about it. I'm sick of talking about it."
>
> YOU: "Ok, but I'm ready to help if you change your mind. If you bring it up again, I

will take it as a sign that you want my help
with it. Otherwise, I won't mention it."

There are many times when your partner won't actually want to work on problem solving. Those times are mainly when he or she was just trying to pick a fight, or when he or she senses some fault in himself or herself. By refusing to join in the fight and by standing by to help, you make it much less likely that your partner is going to bring this subject up again. If you consistently use the agreement method with blaming, your partner will give up trying to provoke a fight this way because it won't work. You will have effectively helped your partner to stop blaming you.

Example: Agreement used when you are at fault

SPOUSE: "You gave me the wrong
information for this year's taxes and because
of that, I have to fill out a whole new set of
tax forms and send them to the government
and pay a penalty. You wasted a lot of my
time and money too."
YOU: "Yes, you are right. I am sorry. What
can I do to help with the refiling?"
SPOUSE: "Nothing. You have done enough
already!"
YOU: "Can I help to pay the penalty or do
something for you to make up for the time it
will take you?"
SPOUSE: "No. Just forget it. I will take care
of it."
YOU: "Ok. But, let me know if there is
something I can do."

Sometimes you will be at fault and you will have caused some trouble to your partner. There's no way around that if you are a human being. When we do something that is wrong, we would like our partner to be sensitive and nice about it, but he or she may not be. If he or she is abusive, then deal with the abuse. Your having done something wrong is no excuse for your partner to abuse you. But, as long as there is no abuse, it's better to ignore your partner's emotions and focus on apologizing and making amends.

Making amends is not a penalty or punishment for something we did wrong. Making amends is somehow reducing the damage that we did. So, if I break your window, making amends may be paying for a new window, installing a new window, or hiring someone else to install a window for you. It would not be making amends for me to mow your lawn or give up my vacation.

It won't always be possible to make amends because we might not possess the skills to help, the money to help, or because there is nothing to be done for the damage. In that case, we still need to apologize and accept any decisions that others make. If we break the law, others may decide to arrest us and jail us. If we have an affair or become addicted to drugs, our spouse may decide to divorce us.

Once amends have been made or justice served (legal consequences), we need to forgive ourselves and also create boundaries around further blame from others. So, if you have done your best to apologize *and* make amends to your spouse, but your spouse continues to blame you, then do not continue to apologize. Continued blaming is an act of vengeance on your partner's part, which is to say it is an attack.

Example: Continuing to be blamed for an event in the distant past

> SPOUSE: *"I can't stop thinking about how you really hurt me and damaged our marriage five years ago."*
> YOU: *"You can forgive me or not. That decision is yours. But, I'm not going to discuss it anymore with you. I have apologized and done what I could to make amends."*

Although you may have caused a lot of damage before, and although it may be hard for your spouse to let it go, continuing to apologize or to pay a penalty is not going to help your relationship. Your spouse has to decide whether to hang onto it or let it go. Your participating in accepting "punishment" for it would be a codependent behavior because it is harmful for your spouse to remain unforgiving. Your spouse may need professional help, or you may need to separate and force the choice of whether your spouse forgives you or not. Love cannot survive without forgiveness.

Be careful also not to "allow" your partner to do damaging behaviors to somehow even the score. Two wrongs never make a right in a relationship. Two wrongs simply cause more damage than one wrong.

You can be blamed for anything—past, present, or future—reality based, or fantasy based. You could be blamed for the moon being round, the behavior of your parents, or your partner's unhappiness, for example. Let's take a look:

Example: Being blamed for something totally unrelated to you

SPOUSE: *"You make me miserable. You make me want to run away from home."*

YOU: *"You do seem pretty unhappy."*

SPOUSE: *"Of course I am, the way that you behave."*

YOU: *"You may be right. Let's take a look at some ways we could make things better for you."*

SPOUSE: *"You've got to change or I am just going to be stuck being miserable."*

YOU: *[taking out a piece of paper and starting problem solving] "That's a good place to start." [you write down the problem as "(Spouse's name) would like to feel happier"] .*

As before, the blaming is not really the important thing, so don't get caught up in fighting about whether you are really to blame or not. That wouldn't accomplish anything. Instead, agree with what you can and transition to problem solving as described in the chapter on problem solving.

And, once again, if your partner refuses the problem solving:

> SPOUSE: *"You make me miserable. You make me want to run away from home."*
> YOU: *"You do seem pretty unhappy."*
> SPOUSE: *"Of course I am, the way that you behave."*
> YOU: *"You may be right. Let's take a look at some ways we could make things better for you."*
> SPOUSE: *"You've got to change or I am just going to be stuck being miserable."*
> YOU: *[taking out a piece of paper and starting problem solving] "That's a good place to start." [you write down the problem as "(Spouse's name) would like to feel happier"]* .
> SPOUSE: *"You can play with your little piece of paper. I'm going out."*
> YOU: *"Ok, if you want to drop it, we will. If you bring it up again, though, I will take that as a cue that you want to work with me on making things better."*
> SPOUSE: *"Take it any way you want."*

You may be thinking, "What does it accomplish to emphasize the cooperative problem solving if my partner won't cooperate?" By agreeing and using problem solving, you take the payoff away from your partner's behavior. He or she blames you, but instead of it bothering you, you take it as an opportunity to positively and cooperatively work together. Not only that, but your partner will learn to *expect* this response from you. He or she will either work with you or stop blaming you. Either way, it is a win-win. Why is it a win for your partner? Because it is harmful for him or her to continue to blame you.

When You Can't Agree with Anything

Throughout this book, I maintain that there is *always* something to agree with. In my 20 years of coaching and counseling, I have yet to hear a statement where I could not help a client to find something to agree with. I have often challenged my clients to blame me for something that they think I would not be able to find any agreement with. Although I have had some very smart clients, none of them has been able to do it. Nevertheless, I will give you a way to respond to blaming when you cannot find anything to agree with.

Example of responding when you can't find anything to agree with:

> *SPOUSE: "You always try to put me down in front of my friends and it is destroying this marriage."*
>
> *YOU: (Totally unaware of what your spouse is talking about) "I didn't realize I was doing that, but maybe I am. Would you help me to understand how I'm doing that?"*

Although you may believe that your spouse is totally wrong, keep in mind that good communication is not about right and wrong. Additionally, all of us have blind spots—aspects of ourselves that we can't see, but others can. If your spouse says something that you think it *totally* wrong, there is a possibility that it is a blind spot issue—something that you are doing, but are unaware of.

There are two possible outcomes when you respond this way. Either your spouse will or will not have examples of your behavior. Whether he or she has examples or not, the outcome will be good when you respond this way.

Example: Nothing to agree with, but your spouse has examples

> **SPOUSE:** *"You always try to put me down in front of my friends and it is destroying this marriage."*
>
> **YOU:** *(Totally unaware of what your spouse is talking about) "I didn't realize I was doing that, but maybe I am. Would you help me to understand how I'm doing that?"*
>
> **SPOUSE:** *"Well, like when you said that we only have a small garden. I work very hard on that garden. Saying 'only' makes it seem very unimportant."*
>
> **YOU:** *"I see what you mean. I am sorry. Thank you for helping me to understand."*

Notice in this example that you don't try to explain that you didn't mean any harm. That is a defensive reaction and not a helpful one. Whether you meant harm or not, harm was done, so apologizing is the best thing to do. It will cost you nothing, but it will benefit your relationship.

Sometimes your spouse won't have any examples. This can happen when he or she has come to a conclusion without evidence. Let's take a look at what that might look like.

Example: Nothing to agree with, and your spouse has no examples

> **SPOUSE:** *"You always try to put me down in front of my friends and it is destroying this marriage."*
>
> **YOU:** *(Totally unaware of what your spouse is talking about) "I didn't realize I was doing that, but maybe I am. Would you help me to understand how I'm doing that?"*
>
> **SPOUSE:** *"I can't think of anything right now, but you always do that."*
>
> **YOU:** *"The next time it happens, please point it out to me. I don't want to make you feel put down."*
>
> **SPOUSE:** *"I will."*
>
> **YOU:** *(nicely) "Thank you."*

If your spouse can't find an example, it is very likely that he or she will drop it and not bring it up again. His or her own search for examples will do the convincing. Although you might feel like telling your spouse that he or she is wrong when he or she can't think of examples, that won't help your relationship. It will give you a little bit of satisfaction at the expense of your spouse. Express your love to your spouse, even when he or she is wrong and your relationship will grow all the more.

Summary

Blaming, complaining, and verbal abuse are three distinct behaviors. Assess clearly and prioritize what you are dealing with. With some partners, it may be all three.

Dealing with verbal abuse always takes priority over dealing with blaming or complaining, even if you are at fault for something. Agreement is not a good intervention for stopping abuse. If you are being physically and/or emotionally abused, get help and deal with that first.

The typical ways of dealing with blaming are defending, counter-blaming, and distancing—all of which are harmful to relationships. Although people feel like they need to defend or explain, defending and explaining only prolong the problem. Although you need to apologize when you are wrong, you don't have to justify yourself when you are right.

Instead of defending and explaining, you can use the agreement method to transform blaming statements your spouse makes into opportunities for connection and cooperation. Even if your spouse refuses to cooperate, the agreement method will discourage his or her continued use of blaming. The method of agreement keeps you in control, in a nice way that doesn't damage your relationship.

♥10♥

USING AGREEMENT FOR BETTER DATES WITH YOUR SPOUSE

Although dates are supposed to be fun, for married people they often aren't. Couples can have conflict because of what they do (or don't do) on dates, but the bigger problem usually has to do with their emotional connection. When a couple are emotionally close, almost anything they do will be fun just because they enjoy being with each other. The more emotionally distant they become, the less they enjoy being with each other—even if the activity normally would be fun. Therefore, the key to improving your dating is to build your emotional connection to your spouse. The method of agreement is ideally suited to doing this.

For the purpose of this book, I define *dating* as going out with your significant other, one on one or with a group of people, for the purpose of having a good time. That definition does allows for the modern definition (in the United States) of dates being sexual, but also allows for dates which are not sexual. So, when I refer to "dating issues," I am not referring to sexual issues. Sexual issues are discussed in the chapter on agreement and selfishness.

People who are having a great relationship generally will not be reading this book and will be off doing something they enjoy with their partner, so I won't concern myself with writing for them. You probably see these people occasionally when you go somewhere and guess that they are either in a new relationship, having an affair, or are just disgusting. It's difficult to see other couples having a great relationship when you are struggling with yours, isn't it?

Making your dates more enjoyable will improve your marriage overall. If you have a specific marital problem other than dating, that will need to be dealt with first. Otherwise, that issue will interfere with dating. Once that is done, you may still need some help to get your dating back on track. This chapter will be useful for couples who have overcome a major problem as well as for couples who have emotionally grown away from each other. Keep in mind that overcoming problems doesn't instantly make us fall in love again. Good dating can help to regrow love.

Types of Dating Differences

Differences don't become arguments or problems until we make them that way. I am convinced that most people make them that way simply because they don't know how else to deal with them—other than to not deal with them at all. And that's no good either. Sticking our head in the sand just gets dirt in our ears and it becomes even harder to communicate.

So what kind of dating differences do people in committed relationships have? They can differ in their desire to date, they can differ in what they want to do on a date, they can differ on how often to date, they can differ on how much money to spend on a date, they can differ on whether to leave the children with a sitter so they can date, they can differ on their desire to include others on the date, they can differ on how to do activities on a date, they can differ on what to talk about on their date, and just about any other thing you can think of about dating. This chapter will help you with all of these differences.

Two Typical Patterns with Dating Problems

With so many things to differ about, and so few ways to deal with differences, it is no wonder that so many couples fall into one of two patterns. They either: 1) don't date, or very rarely date; or 2) always have the same kind of date, which is as predictable as their jobs and about as much fun.

When I work with couples, one of the ways I use to assess their communication is to have them plan a date while I am listening. Typically, they tell me that they have a hard time planning dates, deciding on what to do, and planning the logistics (e.g. how to get there, what to do with the children, etc.). But, when they plan a date in my presence, even for the first time, it usually takes them less than five minutes to both agree on something they would like to do and to arrange the logistics. It amazes them. They say they can never do that on their own. Yet, they did it on their own in my office or on the phone with me. The only thing I contributed was listening or reminding them to also arrange the logistics.

It seems that when they try to plan dates on their own, they get sidetracked and argue, or else give up. When they plan in front of me, they remain focused and positive. And, that's without me even teaching them anything! Intuitively they know how to plan a date, but have gotten in a habit of not making an effort at being focused and positive.

The way you communicate about something is every bit as important as the subject you are talking about. Argue about something and your relationship becomes worse. Talk about the same thing with focus, agreement, and loving words, and your relationship will get better. You can use this as your own personal challenge to improve *any* area of your relationship by talking about it in a different way—a more focused, positive, and agreeable way.

Typical Problems in Date Planning

It might help you to learn better if I compare ineffective and effective approaches and point out the differences. First, I will share with you some of my observations of how people often handle dating differences. Then, I will share with you better ways.

There are many different variations of date planning and your way is likely to be a little different from these. The thing to pay attention to is whether your way contains the elements that are effective in resolving differences. Also, be careful to notice if there are things that you are doing that are ineffective and cause more distance in your relationship. If you do find some areas where you are currently ineffective, you will have already taken a step forward. And, like a bone in your grilled fish, you can pick it out before your relationship chokes on it.

Deferring

Deferring is simply agreeing with whatever your spouse wants, without adding any real input of your own.

Example of deferring:
SPOUSE: "Where would you like to go to dinner tonight?"
YOU: "I don't care. Where do you want to go?"

Although this doesn't seem like a conflict situation, it often leads to conflict. There are a few problems with this approach: 1) it shows little enthusiasm to go out with your spouse; 2) if you really do care where you go, your spouse will have to "guess" where you actually want to go; and 3) it can become irritating to have a spouse who never makes choices. On the other hand, if you only use this response once in a while, it will probably be fine. Your being decisive at other times will encourage your spouse to make an honest decision this time.

Another example of deferring:
SPOUSE: "After dinner, would you like to take a walk along the river?"

YOU: "If you want to."

You can kind of feel the lack of enthusiasm in this response, can't you? It's not really agreement. Agreement would be more like, "Yes, I would." Deferring is very passive and low energy. It's easy to imagine a depressed person using this style of responding or date planning.

Complaining

As with blaming, complaining is generally done by people who are not happy. It can be an effort to bring someone else down to an equal level of unhappiness. It can also be an attempt to improve another person by pointing out all of their errors and hoping that will make them do better next time—much like a school teacher might point out all the mistakes on a spelling test. Unfortunately, it tends to be discouraging rather than helpful. It makes people tend to give up rather than try harder.

Example of complaining in date planning:

YOU: "Would you like to go to the new chicken place that opened up last week?"

SPOUSE: "No, it will be too crowded because everyone wants to try it now."

YOU: "Well, how about our usual Italian restaurant?"

SPOUSE: "No, I'm tired of eating the same old thing."

YOU: "Well, where would you like to go?"

SPOUSE: "I don't care. Just not the new chicken place or the Italian place."

YOU: "Ok, I know, let's get some seafood at the family seafood restaurant."

SPOUSE: "Oh, good, another noisy dinner in a brightly lit restaurant."

> *YOU: "If you don't like that, then where do you want to go? I'm not going to make any more suggestions!"*
> *SPOUSE: "Ok, ok. The Italian restaurant, I guess."*
> *YOU: "I thought you didn't want to eat the same old thing?"*
> *SPOUSE: "That's true, but it's better than eating in a bright room full of screaming kids."*

On the surface this looks like debating, but it's not actually debating at all. In debating, your spouse would also provide her own ideas and defend them as well as attack your ideas. This is actually complaining because your spouse points out the reasons why your choices are bad ones while offering none of her own.

In a debate, it is possible to lose. But the complainer never loses. This is because he or she doesn't provide his or her own choices. A one-sided win is also guaranteed if the complainer later finds fault with whatever was chosen ("I knew this place wouldn't be any good"). This pattern will lead to an end to dating much faster than deferring will. It creates a negative atmosphere right from the beginning of the date which has to be overcome if you are going to be able to have a good time.

Debating

Debating is the fall back method I mention throughout this book, which has to do with each partner promoting his or her ideas while putting the other partner's ideas down. It is an attempt by each partner to prove that not only are his or her ideas better, but his or her spouse's ideas are problematic or maybe just plain dumb.

Example of debating in date planning:

YOU: "How about going out with Ben and Cindy this weekend? We could get some drinks and have a few laughs."

SPOUSE: "Ben and Cindy? Those morons? Their idea of a good time is telling dirty jokes and farting. Let's go out with my friends for a change. "

YOU: "Like who?"

SPOUSE: "Like Rachel and Michael. They're really nice and we haven't seen them for a long time."

YOU: "There's a reason for that. Michael doesn't know anything about sports and I'm not interested in tax law. So, we just end up listening to you and Rachel talk all night. What a bore."

SPOUSE: "You could talk about something other than sports. There is more happening in the world than sports, you know."

YOU: "Like what? What people are wearing? Or who was the latest guest on Oprah? No thanks."

Debates can't go on endlessly because people run out of energy eventually. They often end in compromise or in not doing anything. With debating, it becomes harder and harder to bring up new ideas and so couples soon fall into a dating routine. That resolves the conflict, but as time goes on, the dates feel more like an obligation, talking stops, or focuses on business, and the couple feel relieved when the date is over. Feeling better about ending a date than you do about going on a date is a sure sign of problems.

Demanding

Demanding is using power in an attempt to get compliance. It is vertical communication, top-down, from a superior to a subordinate. Like all people with authority, demanding people gain their power only by the cooperation of those under them. If the other person does not comply, usually the demanding person will attempt to use even more power in order to maintain dominance. This means that this kind of communication has the possibility of escalating to a verbally or even physically abusive situation.

Fortunately, most people have an internal boundary which prevents them from becoming abusive. When they reach the level where they are at risk for losing self control, they usually just end the conversation.

Example of demanding in date planning:

SPOUSE: "I've decided what we are going to do this weekend. We are going to a car show. Make sure you are ready at 6:00 a.m. on Saturday, because we have to leave early."

YOU: "I'm not really interested in going to a car show."

SPOUSE: "Did I ask you if you are interested? I said that is what we are doing, so I don't want to hear any more about it."

YOU: "Well, ok, but I'm not going."

SPOUSE: "Oh, no? You always try to undermine my attempts to make life better for us. If you don't go, then you can forget me doing any more activities with you, and you can pay for your own activities by yourself."

There are two typical responses to demands. One is *compliance*, which is saying "yes" without any boundaries at all.

The other is *refusing,* which is all boundary with no loving message at all.

Compliance, or giving in to demands, prevents conflict but encourages the demanding behavior to continue. Refusing can quickly lead to no dating at all. The relationship becomes worse either way. Either it becomes worse from the conflict that happens when you refuse, or it becomes worse from the growing resentment of giving in to unreasonable demands.

The "or else" quality of demands is very effective when used with an insecure spouse. An insecure spouse is one who is afraid of what would happen if the relationship ended. Many people marry someone who rescues them from needy feelings or an impoverished situation. They then find themselves in marriages where they are on the lower end of all communication. If you have ever seen a woman with a partner who treats her very badly, the number one reason will be that she needs her partner so much that she will put up with anything. Love does not tolerate behaviors which damage the relationship, but neediness does.

In such cases, more than agreement and boundaries will be needed to really improve the relationship. What will be required is gaining the ability to be independent financially and emotionally—to practically become less needy. When we depend on someone to emotionally or physically take care of us, we give them the ability to make unreasonable demands of us. A nice spouse won't do that, but there are plenty who will.

Avoiding

Avoiding is a way of refusing without saying "no." It is often used by passive, as well as passive aggressive people.

Example of avoidance in date planning:
YOU: "Honey, there's a really good movie out. Would you like to go see it with me?"
SPOUSE: "I guess so. It might be fun."
YOU: "Ok, how about Friday night?
SPOUSE: "Friday night? Ok, that's fine."
[Friday comes]

> **YOU:** *"I'm really looking forward to going to the movie with you tonight."*
>
> **SPOUSE:** *"Oh, I'm sorry, my boss gave me an extra project and I can't go. I'll make it up to you some other time, ok?"*
>
> **YOU:** *"I was really looking forward to going to the movie with you tonight. We agreed on it."*
>
> **SPOUSE:** *"I know, but what can I do? I would rather go to a movie than work, too. This job really stinks sometimes, but we've got to pay the bills."*
>
> **YOU:** *"I know. Well, maybe some other time."*

People who avoid always have a reason for avoiding. They don't say, "The reason I didn't meet you is because I was avoiding going out with you." If an avoidant person could be aware and open like that, he or she wouldn't be avoidant. If you get angry with avoidant people, they will just point out how unfair you are since they could not help canceling, being late, forgetting, getting sick, etc. If you agree with the avoidant person without using boundaries, then the behavior continues—building resentment and a sense of futility ("what's the use of asking...?") that undermines the relationship. So, just as with a demanding partner, improving the relationship depends on a combination of agreement and boundaries. Either one alone will not have the desired results. I will give you some examples of how to do this later in this chapter.

Derailing During a Date

The section above talked about common communication problems in date *planning,* including deferring, debating, complaining, demanding, and avoiding. In addition to these date planning problems, there is another kind of problem that can happen once you are on a date. Derailing is an expression from the railroad industry and refers to a train going off the tracks. It is a potentially disastrous situation, much like crash landing an airplane.

Derailing in dating is when something happens during the date to significantly change the mood or purpose of the date—from one of emotional connection to emotional disconnection. In a healthy relationship, people sometimes say or do the wrong thing, but they are both able to catch the situation before it gets out of hand and to stay on track. One partner may make a careless or critical remark which momentarily upsets the other. Then he or she apologizes, the partner lets it go (both verbally and mentally), and they shift the conversation to something positive. The incident is left behind like a pothole which was struck several miles ago and has quickly been forgotten.

Example of how to avoid derailing on a date:
YOU: "Wow, you really look nice tonight."
SPOUSE: "It's nice of you to notice for a change."
YOU: "Forget I said anything. I want to have a good time tonight."
SPOUSE: "Sorry, guess I said that wrong."
YOU: "Did you say something? I forgot already (smiling)."
[The couple continues with their date in a positive mood]

One thing to be aware of is that you need to not only say nice things, but you need to say nice things *nicely.* Your tone and facial expression can be even more important than the words you use.

In a stressed or strained relationship, or in a new relationship, the same kind of slip up can cause derailing. The partner that slipped up may not apologize, the apology may not be accepted, or the apology is verbally accepted, but not mentally. A dark cloud forms over the couple who then must be very careful not to add anything more to it, lest it become a storm. With a very stressed couple, the storm can happen right from the first wrong comment and the date can be unsalvageable.

Example of derailing on a date:

YOU: "Wow, you really look nice tonight."
SPOUSE: "It's nice of you to notice for a change."
YOU: "What's that supposed to mean? I always notice, but you usually look like crap."
SPOUSE: "You know what, I changed my mind about going out tonight."
YOU: "Fine with me. I've got better things to do, anyhow."
[Couple returns home in a bad mood]

As you will see later in this chapter, the method of agreement is very helpful for preventing derailing when such slip-ups happen. The method of agreement can also be used with more intentional derailing, such as the following:

Example of deliberate derailing:

SPOUSE: "This place really stinks. You made a pretty bad choice when you picked this place. I wish I had stayed home."

If your partner is deliberately trying to derail the date, the method of agreement will not be enough without boundaries. And, if things go beyond complaining or criticism to verbal abuse, you will need to use boundaries without agreement.

Dating is another one of those situations in which you have to be careful not to allow any verbal abuse (a zero tolerance policy is best). If verbal abuse happens on your date, end the date *immediately*. Take a taxi home if you need to, but do not accept an apology. If someone punches you in the face and then apologized, would you say it was ok? Of course not. Treat verbal abuse the same as physical abuse or it will get worse.

The Purpose of Dating

To get the most out of dating, it's important to remember the purpose of dating. Too often we get caught up in details that are trivial, or we put more emphasis on the activity than the relationship. When we take the time and energy to take care of the relationship first, our dates will go better no matter the activity, and we will look forward to continued dates. Dating should always be planned with the relationship in mind first, the activity a distant second.

Another reason to put the relationship first in all date planning is because the purpose of dating, in a committed relationship, is to enhance the relationship. It compensates for the wear and tear of daily routine. Dating should break up the routine, rather than be a part of the routine. It should add vibrancy, variety, and interest to the relationship. One thing that attracts people to affairs is the excitement and freshness that comes with a new relationship. But, there is no reason that we can't intentionally build excitement and freshness into our existing relationship.

The smallest of changes can create the feeling of newness in dating. Changes don't have to be costly in terms of time or money, but if you can afford it, things that take time and money are also great. In my early years, I often had more time than money, so I learned to love camping, hiking, picnicking (cheaper than a restaurant and just as romantic) and many other low cost activities. My wife didn't know much about these activities when I met her, but has come to love them through my consistently positive attitude and desire to make these things enjoyable for her. Although we can afford to do more now, those cheaper dates remain some of our favorites.

Many couples complain that because of their different interests, it is hard to find a variety of activities that they both enjoy. A simple solution to that is to combine elements that you both like into the same date. If he likes to golf and she likes to eat at new restaurants, they can have a weekly golf-restaurant outing. If she doesn't know how to play golf, the first dates can be spent learning together. Or, she can take some lessons on her own. I took two courses to be able to enjoy my wife's interests more. One was in understanding and listening to classical music, and the other was in learning how to appreciate great paintings. Museums used to bore me, but no longer. And, now I enjoy listening to classical music on my mp3 player.

For couples who really can't find a way to combine their interests, they can take turns choosing the date—picking what they like without regard for their partner's interests. This usually works well because there is no need to discuss (argue about?) what they are going to do and attitudes stay positive on the date. How can a partner's attitudes stay positive on a date when he or she doesn't like the activity? It's not so hard because he knows that next time, they will be doing what he likes (and *vice versa*).

What if your partner chooses something like sky diving and that really scares you (I am married to such a daredevil wife)? Do it if you can, at least once before you say it is terrible. And, if you just can't, then go as an assistant to your partner. Make the lunch, cheer, take pictures, push him or her out of the plane, etc. Do the part that you *can* do with a positive attitude. It will make a big difference. Instead of trying to convince your partner that something is a terrible idea, let the activity either convince your partner or you. Some things my wife thought she was going to hate, she actually liked. And me, too.

Using the Method of Agreement to Improve Dating

In this section, I want to tell you how to deal with the five problems of deferring, complaining, debating, demanding, and complaining. I think you know that if you are doing these things, then you need to knock it off and get with the program. Helping your spouse to enjoy dates means helping your spouse to enjoy you and that is good for you, too. And, if your spouse has these behaviors, you can use the method of agreement to change things for the better.

Agreement with a deferring partner

Deferring is a way of avoiding responsibility or thinking. I think it is somewhat similar to the person who never initiates sex, but who is receptive to his or her partner's initiations. The main thing to do here is to not have an expectation that your spouse needs to be the one to decide. If he or she has a positive attitude and you have a good time, then be the one to choose. Keep in mind that if your spouse did choose, it might be something that you wouldn't like. In other words, let not choosing the activity be your spouse's problem instead of your own. If he or she doesn't like your choices, he or she can speak up. If he or she complains about your choices, then see the section on agreement with a complaining partner.

Example of agreement with a deferring spouse:
YOU: "Do you have any preference for what we do on our date this weekend?"
SPOUSE: "I don't care. Whatever you want to do."
YOU: "Really? That's great. You're the best. This weekend I want to take you on a new bicycle trail I discovered near my workplace."
SPOUSE: "Ok, but I'm not sure how well I will do..."
YOU: "Hey, that's ok. We'll have fun no matter how we do. And if we don't, no big deal. This time is just an experiment."
SPOUSE: "Ok, then."

Because a person who defers is really agreeing with you, the only thing for you to agree with is your spouse's agreeing! That's just about as easy as it gets in the way of agreement. Don't play into any lack of enthusiasm on your spouse's part, because that will only reward that behavior. Try to think like a man who really wants to have sex. If she doesn't say "no," then it's a "go," but he better make sure she enjoys it too or it will turn out to be a one hit wonder experience ("We did it one time and never again...I wonder what happened?").

Agreement with a complaining partner

You can help yourself and your partner by helping him or her to gradually give up a complaining style of communication. Most communication is habit and the words that come out of our mouths the easiest are the ones which we have said the most. What this means for you is that your partner's complaining is a habit, and it is going to take time to change that habit. When you are using agreement, keep that in mind.

Example of agreement with a complaining spouse:

YOU: "Would you like to go to the new chicken place that opened up last week?"

SPOUSE: "No, it will be too crowded because everyone wants to try it now."

YOU: "Yes, that's true. I didn't think of that. Well, where do you think would be good to go?"

SPOUSE: "I don't know. You pick a place."

YOU: "I will do that if you want. But, if you complain about it, then I am not going to pick any more and I will leave it to you to decide."

SPOUSE: "I wasn't complaining, I was just pointing out the facts."

YOU: "Ok, your way of saying it may be better. I will pick a place and if you point out negative facts about it, I will leave it to you to decide."

SPOUSE: "If you are going to be that way, then I'm not going out at all."

YOU: "Ok. Thank you for deciding. We can go some other time if you like."
SPOUSE: "There won't be another time. I'm through going out with you."
YOU: "Ok. Thanks for letting me know."

Does this sound really bad to you? Certainly it's a date killer the first time or two you go through this routine, but it will put an end to the pattern of complaining. What the complainer wants is to gain control over your emotions. By being agreeable, the complainer gets control over where to go or not go, but does not gain control over your emotions. In other words, complaining goes from being a way to control your emotions to being a kind of self punishment for the complainer. He or she has cheated himself or herself out of going out. If you argue, this won't work. Let your partner's complaining be his or her problem—not yours. Let it cause problems for your partner—not you. I also recommend that you go out on your own and have a good time.

People who complain a lot don't only do it about dating, but about nearly everything else as well. A combination of agreement and boundaries can help them to change. Of course, in the process of changing, they will blame you for their having to be "careful" of what they say. Although you may not like to hear it, essentially they are correct. They do need to be careful about what they say. That is what socialized people do in a relationship. If your partner is not being careful about what he or she says, it means that your boundaries are not strong enough. It does not mean that you need to argue or directly try to change your partner. Those ways won't work.

Since your boundaries have to be strong in order to change the communication of a complainer, it is equally important that you be loving every chance you get when they are not complaining. For a person who is a *habitual* complainer, two weeks of this kind of behavior on your part can really help to improve the relationship. If your partner only *occasionally* complains, it may take a few months to change this behavior. But, in both cases, you do it by setting boundaries, being agreeable, being loving, and being consistent. If your spouse is a habitual complainer and after two weeks the communication pattern has not improved, I recommend getting marriage or relationship coaching. Habitual complaining puts out the fires of love and can take a relationship to the point where it is very hard to get the love burning again.

The typical approach of complaining to the complainer is like trying to put out a fire with a fire. The number one obstacle to people who are helping their partner to stop complaining is the expectation that their partner can change in one day. Get rid of any such expectations. Instead, expect your partner to continue to complain and to only gradually develop the ability to think before speaking. It's likely that he or she has had the habit of complaining for many years. Don't take it personally. See what you are doing as helping. If your children are complainers, you will also want to use similar boundaries with them, except with them, they will learn faster.

Agreeing with a debating partner

Debating is similar to problem solving in that you are both coming up with reasons for and against doing something. It is unlike problem solving in that you both have already come to the conclusion about what is the best choice. In counseling, this is known as "foreclosure," or coming to a decision before all the facts have been considered. Once decided, people defend their position even in light of contradictory evidence. What will really help to end debating is to move all debates toward problem solving. To do that, you need to agree and guide, rather than suddenly throw out your ideas and opinions.

Example of agreement with a debating spouse:
YOU: "How about going out with Ben and Cindy this weekend? We could get some drinks and have a few laughs."
SPOUSE: "Ben and Cindy? Those morons? Their idea of a good time is telling dirty jokes and farting. Let's go out with my friends for a change. "

> *YOU: "I can see we have some different ideas and we could fight about it, but I'm not going to do that. I want us to be close and have a good time. Maybe you are right and it really wouldn't be good to go out with Ben and Cindy this weekend."*
>
> *SPOUSE: "Well, I have an idea. How about going out with Rachel and Michael?"*
>
> *YOU: "That might be a good idea. Let's sit down and consider all the possibilities before we decide."*
>
> *SPOUSE: "Huh?"*
>
> *YOU: "Yes, come here. I will show you how we can decide in a good way without arguing."*
>
> *SPOUSE: "Ok, but I'm not going out with Ben and Cindy."*
>
> *YOU: "Understood, loud and clear. I won't fight you on it."*
>
> *SPOUSE: "Ok."*
>
> *YOU: [Move into problem solving with, "Go out and have a good time together this weekend," as the identified problem].*

Most people hate argument and will follow you into a "problem solving mode" as long as you agree that there are some really good aspects of what they are saying. For example, if you don't have a lot of money, but your spouse suggests staying overnight in a luxury hotel, then tell her (or him) that sounds like a lot of fun, but that you want to sit down and think it out to make sure it would be the best for both of you. Then shift into problem solving (see the chapter on problem solving).

Any debates that can't be resolved with problem solving either need to be put away ("agree to disagree'), or require extra help. If you start to build up a lot of these "agree to disagree" topics, then it will be time for professional help.

Using the method of agreement with a demanding partner

Not many people want their spouse to be like their commanding officer. The goal of using agreement in dealing with a demanding partner is to establish equal levels of authority. You don't want to gain authority over your spouse, as that wouldn't be making things equal—it simply would be reversing roles, with you being in command instead of your partner. Getting to an equal level of authority means you each have control over yourself so that you can work together.

Example of agreement with a demanding partner:

SPOUSE: *"I've decided what we are going to do this weekend. We are going to a car show. Make sure you are ready at 6:00 a.m. on Saturday, because we have to leave early."*

YOU: *"Yes, a car show is one thing we could do this weekend and it might be fun. But, I am going to consider all of my options before making a decision."*

SPOUSE: *"What do you mean? Didn't you hear me? I already said we are going to a car show."*

YOU: *"Yes, I heard you. You said we are going to a car show and you want me to be ready at 6:00 a.m. on Saturday. Is there some other part that I missed?"*

SPOUSE: *"No, but there is nothing else to decide."*

YOU: *"Yes, you have made your decision, and I respect that. And I may decide to go*

with you. If you try to force me to, then I
won't go. But, if you want to sit down with
me and help me to consider all the options
first, then I may decide to go with you."

What I want you to notice here is that there is no direct refusal to do what your spouse is wanting. What your spouse wants may be good or bad, but getting into an argument about that would miss the point. The point is not about deciding on the best activity, but on ending the bossy style of communication. You use a boundary not to refuse the activity, but to refuse the way it is expressed to you. As long as your spouse is willing to decide *with* you rather than *for* you, you will consider the merits of his or her idea.

Just as with changing other communication, don't expect to change everything in one verbal exchange. You may get to the problem solving on the first attempt, but are more likely to end up just refusing to go. That's ok. Missing whatever activity it is will be worth the relationship improvement for you and your spouse, once the change has been made. The most important thing is being consistent *without* being argumentative. If you argue with an authoritarian person, not only will you lose, but it is likely to escalate and cause more damage.

After you use this method for a while (longer for only occasionally bossy spouses), the bossiness will end and you will both be making decisions together. Once your spouse comes to like the problem solving process, you may be surprised at how often he or she wants to use it for discussing a variety of things. Do your best to participate, because if the problem solving stops working, he or she will go back to being demanding.

Using the method of agreement with an avoidant partner

Like the demanding person, the avoidant person is also exercising a kind of control. You can feel how much power he or she has when your dates are canceled or when your spouse is habitually late. If you get upset at such behavior, your spouse will have made you a victim by his or her behavior. Your agreement and boundaries need to help your spouse to victimize only himself or herself, if anyone at all. In other words, when he or she cancels, it will hurt him or her and not you. When he or she is late, it will hurt him or her and not you. When such emotional power over you is gone, the avoidant behavior will stop.

Example of using agreement with an avoidant spouse:

> *YOU: "Honey, there's a really good movie out. Would you like to go see it with me?"*
>
> *SPOUSE: "I guess so. It might be fun."*
>
> *YOU: "Ok, how about Friday night?*
>
> *SPOUSE: "Friday night? Ok, that's fine."*
>
> *YOU: "Good, I will plan on that. But, I will also make a plan to go out with a friend in case something comes up and you can't make it."*
>
> *SPOUSE: "I told you Friday is fine. You can count on me."*
>
> *[Friday comes]*
>
> *YOU: "I'm really looking forward to going to the movie with you tonight."*
>
> *SPOUSE: "Oh, I'm sorry, my boss gave me an extra project and I can't go. I'll make it up to you some other time, ok?"*
>
> *YOU: "Don't worry about it. I have my backup plans. Don't work too hard and you don't have to wait up for me."*
>
> *SPOUSE: "What, you are going out without me? That's not fair that I have to work while you get to go out and have fun."*

> *YOU: "Yes, you are right. It isn't fair. But,*
> *it's important."*
> *SPOUSE: "Important for what?"*
> *YOU: "I would be happy to talk to you about*
> *it, but not right now. I have to get ready.*
> *When would you like to talk about it?"*
> *SPOUSE: "I don't know."*
> *YOU: "No problem. Just let me know*
> *anytime you want to talk about it. I love*
> *you. See you later."*

What I want you to notice in this example is that there is no arguing or complaining to your spouse. You agree that his or her reasons for canceling are important. You don't complain about it, and you don't try to find some way for your spouse to not have to cancel. That is your spouse's problem—not yours. It may be that your spouse can miraculously find a way to join you after all. If not, he or she will soon learn to keep your dates. Avoidant partners don't care if you don't have fun, but avoidant partners do care if you have fun without them.

For a partner who is perpetually late (more often than is reasonable), you can easily deal with that too.

Example of agreement with a perpetually late spouse:

> *SPOUSE: "I will meet you in front of the mall*
> *at 7:00 pm (or, I'll be home by 7:00)."*
> *YOU: "Ok. But, I know that things*
> *sometimes come up. So, if you are not there*
> *(or not here) by 7:15, I will assume that you*
> *had to change your plans and I will carry on*
> *without you."*

If you have a friend or relative like this, it will also work wonders with them. Not right away, of course. The first couple times it happens, they will complain to other people about how unreasonable you are. But, after that they will meet you on time, every time. They don't really want to be left out.

Using the method of agreement to prevent derailing

If your spouse is deliberately trying to end your date, this method won't work very well since he or she can escalate derailing behaviors to the point where the best thing to do is to end the date. For example, he or she might escalate to verbal abuse, in which case the most important thing for you to do would be to end the date immediately.

However, in relationships which are under stress, but where neither of you wants it to be that way, then the method of agreement can be helpful. It can change the habit of disagreeing and arguing during dates to one of cooperation. Cooperation is an important step on the path to having a good time.

Example of using agreement with accidentally derailing comments:

YOU: "Wow, you really look nice tonight."
SPOUSE: "It's nice of you to notice for a change."
YOU: "Yes, I probably don't tell you enough. But, I think you are really handsome (pretty, sexy, etc.)."
SPOUSE: "Thanks."

There is no need to argue or defend against your spouse's irritation. This remark came out of his or her mouth because of the stress in the relationship. When you use agreement like this, you let some of the stress off—making it less likely that your spouse will say the same thing in the future. Arguing or defending, or just being silent, would increase the stress and make it even more likely that your spouse will either say the same thing in the future or say nothing at all.

Example of agreement with a deliberate derailment attempt:

SPOUSE: "This place really stinks. You made a pretty bad choice when you picked this place. I wish I had stayed home."

YOU: "I agree with you, I thought it would be nicer, too. Maybe we can still turn things around."

SPOUSE: "What do you mean?"

YOU: [Picking up a napkin to write on and starting problem solving] "We both want to have a better time than we are, right?"

SPOUSE: "Yeah."

YOU: [Writing down, "Both want to have a better time" as the agreed on problem]. "Let's brainstorm some ideas...."

Problem solving isn't just for formal meetings. It can be used almost anytime and anywhere. For example, you can use it with your child who is afraid of a monster in the closet:

"We both want you to feel safe, right? What are some things you can do if you are feeling scared?"

And, you can use it when your mom wants you to visit every day:

"We both want to have a good relationship. Let's consider some ways that might work well or not work so well for both of us."

And, with your spouse, when he or she gets irritable or disappointed on a date (as above). Agreement and problem solving both prevents arguments and improves relationships.

I recommend that whenever you use problem solving that you try to do it on paper (even with a young child you can draw pictures as options). Follow the format that is in the problem solving chapter until it becomes second nature to you. It may literally stop you from ever having to argue with anyone again (although I would guess that you really don't *have to* argue with anyone, anyhow).

Troubleshooting

What should I do when my spouse is critical and I don't feel like agreeing or using problem solving?

I never feel like flossing my teeth, but I do. There are many things that we don't want to do that are worth doing anyhow. Another way to look at it is that the alternatives are even harder on us. If we don't do those important but necessary things with our personal goals, our jobs, and our relationships, we will be unhappy, unemployed, alone, and possibly toothless. My suggestion is to go with your feelings when they prompt you to do good things and to use reasoning when you feel an urge to do something harmful to yourself or someone else. Use the correct "brain tool" to get the results you want.

We don't date anymore. How can I use the method of agreement to restart the dating?

As long as you are still communicating, you can deal with the dating as an option (one of the brainstorming ideas) in problem solving something else. For example, if you are problem solving "Wanting to get along better," then one of the brainstorming ideas might be dating. You can then consider the pros and cons of dating. That would be a preliminary step to planning a date. The number of steps to reach a goal depends on how close you are to a goal. It doesn't matter how far away from the goal you are now. It only matters that each step you take brings you closer to what you want to happen.

I have used this technique and it helped some, but the date still wasn't very good. Any suggestions?

Congratulations on making improvement! The fact that it helped shows you are on the right track. Just like climbing a flight of stairs, progress happens one step at a time. If it takes several dates using this method before you can reach the next level, that is ok. Without using this method, you would either have many bad dates or stop dating altogether. You did well—keep it up!

Summary

The quality of your dates is the pulse of your relationship even more than your sexual relationship is. Relationships start to go downhill when dating stops, when dates become routine, or when stress from our personal lives or relationship enters into our dates. Using the method of agreement, we can change the mood of the dating, have dates that we enjoy more, and have less stress. Good dating also helps to "affair proof" your marriage by providing the same benefits an affair would, but in an appropriate way.

I have enough money to last me the rest of my life, unless I buy something.

Jackie Mason
US Comedian

Money is better than poverty, if only for financial reasons.

Woody Allen
US Movie Actor, Comedian, and Director

♥11♥

USING AGREEMENT TO END FINANCIAL CONFLICT AND GET OUT OF DEBT

Are financial problems rational problems to be worked out, or are they relational problems? Actually, they are both and you need to deal with both aspects to keep your relationship strong. Would you agree that arguing is the best way to accomplish this? Can you imagine a financial counselor saying,

> *"I can see that there is a real inequity in your relationship. One of you makes and spends most of the money, but you both do a lot of work. I suggest you go home and argue until this problem is straightened out."*

A little hard to imagine isn't it? That's because you know that arguing will make your relationship worse without making your financial problems any better. The more people argue, the less they are inclined to share what they have or to work as partners. And, if they argue enough, they will create so much distance in their relationship that they will no longer want to be with each other. Like a hurricane, financial problems grow more intense with each added storm. The combination of financial problems and emotional stress can completely wipe out a relationship.

185

Types of Financial Conflict in Relationships

There are four basic things we can do with money. We can acquire it, save it, invest it, or spend it. These are the same areas where couples have conflict.

Low Income Conflicts

Few people complain that their spouse is earning too much money. It's never hard to get rid of excess money, if there is such a thing. A spouse who has a low paying job, no matter how hard he or she is working, may receive complaints about the small paycheck. His or her spouse may also become resentful because he or she has to also work or work extra to make up for the small paycheck. And, not so uncommonly, a person may leave a spouse who does not make much money.

The line from paycheck to complaints to divorce isn't always straight. It may not be the paycheck per se that causes the upset. In fact even if a partner is satisfied, the couple still may end up in conflict. Why? Because the person with the low paying job is not satisfied with his or her own income and feels helpless to change it. A man or woman who can't adequately provide for the needs and desires of his or her family, or meet his or her own standards, may become depressed and irritable, disinterested in going on low cost or no cost dates, spend much of his or her time worried about finances, lose his or her sexual desire, become obsessed with money, and become depressed and withdrawn.

People who can't live up to their own financial standards may choose to suffer alone with their problems, but there is no such thing as suffering alone in a relationship. Self-imposed suffering actually ends up causing suffering for other family members. It is difficult to have to struggle with paying for the basics, but it is a lot harder to do so when your spouse has detached from you and the children. Some way is needed to put partnership back into this situation regardless of income. Such a reconnection is only possible when you use the method of agreement.

There are also some spouses who are more practical than romantic and who do not wish to stay in a relationship with a husband or wife who is not earning (what they consider to be) enough money. Not everyone marries for love, and in relationships that have a history of problems, people are not staying married for love. Many simply stay in their marriage because they don't see a way to financially take care of themselves otherwise.

If their spouse loses his or her job, takes a large pay cut, or causes some problem that takes most of the finances (a health condition, gambling, alcoholism, etc.), divorce may follow soon after. This is much more likely to happen in relationships that lack a romantic connection. The money motive (actually a security motive) also explains why many people stay in relationships which have no romantic connection, even when their spouses have affairs, addictions, or abusive behavior. Their spouse brings home enough money for them to feel it is mentally and physically worth it.

Ironically, it is those who most fear losing their financial support who are most likely to lose it. Arguing about finances makes relationships more distant, which makes them more susceptible to the stress of financial problems. In the midst of this marital distress, if one of the partners manages to become more financially independent, that may trigger a divorce. Or, if the income drops below a certain level, the level of difficulty in the relationship may no longer be worth it to one or both of them and again a divorce may be triggered. This phenomenon is not limited to the lower economic class. Even within the upper economic class, partners can be dissatisfied with the amount of *disposable* income. Some people really do have to give their spouses a lot of money or they will leave. It can be a very expensive investment with little return. At an emotional level it's not surprising that someone would tire of being a "sugar daddy" or "sugar mommy," no matter how good their relationship appears to be doing, and whether they have a marriage license or not.

The common difficulty for all low income problems is the *lack of emotional connection* between partners. While people think an increased income is the answer to their problems, even that won't help in the long run if there is no deliberate work on building an emotional connection. Fortunately, the method of agreement can help with that.

Money Saving and Investing Conflicts

Everyone likes to save money, right? Not right. Everyone likes to have savings available, but most people don't like to save. It takes discipline. It means choosing to do without something now, so that we can have money available for later. And, if we are saving for retirement, it may be much later.

Can you imagine what it would be like to be married to someone who wants to put a major portion of the income into investment or retirement savings, if you didn't believe your marriage would continue to retirement? Or if you didn't think that you would be able to enjoy the money as much as a senior as you could now? Or, if you believed that you would no longer be in good health in your senior years? Or, if you were planning to end your relationship at some point because you were losing more and more of your feelings of love for your spouse? While you could potentially recover money at the time of divorce, you could also end up losing more of it. It might go to spousal support and child support payments. Many a man has saved money for retirement only to lose it when his wife divorced him. Restarting is expensive. Even if you are a woman, you can understand your husband's fear of that.

Even people who agree that they need to save money or invest money still have disagreements over how the money should be saved/invested, how much money should be saved/invested, and when the money can be accessed. Consulting with a financial planner is great for getting information, but won't necessarily resolve these conflicts. That's because the choices are related to the amount of risk that people feel comfortable with as well as their willingness to give up money they could use now for money they could use later. To a large extent these decisions involve guesswork and subjective judgments. Seeing a financial manager can help to make sure that the necessities are taken care of. For example, everyone needs to eat in the future. Everyone needs to have a place to live, and to take care of their health. Beyond these necessities, there are many differences in lifestyle.

It's also possible for a husband or wife to be unaware or insensitive to the security needs or life quality needs of the other. At the extreme, people *could* live on canned beans while they put all of their joint disposable income into a retirement fund, but it is very unlikely that after living on beans for many years that there would still be a couple left to enjoy the money. Clearly, there has to be a balance among the needs of today, our needs and our spouse's needs, and our needs for the future.

The Danger of Not Saving

If there is not enough income to support living for today and saving for tomorrow, usually saving is sacrificed. People are pretty good at living in denial and not thinking about the future. But, when there are no savings, any crisis can drive a couple into bankruptcy. In families where there are no savings, crises can bring about debt and poverty, with all its resulting stress and conflict. Marriages which are already weak can't take the strain.

Without savings, people have to be very careful to anticipate irregular bills such as insurance payments, tax payments, and car replacement. Otherwise they must borrow money each time these expenses come along. Credit cards get used "because we have no choice," and the debt treadmill starts moving more quickly. Running on a debt treadmill where people have to work harder and harder just to pay interest and fees drains our loving feelings and our happiness.

The Method of Agreement Is Not Enough

I don't believe the solution to these problems is simply to use the method of agreement. Clearly, decisions must be made about what the needs of today and tomorrow are, how much savings are needed, how to invest, when to take money from savings and investments, as well as deciding on the lifestyle couples want to have in the future. There is plenty of room here for disagreement and argument, but there is also an opportunity here for agreement and connection. Using the method of agreement in combination with good financial planning and money management can have very practical results as well as very positive emotional results. Being debt free goes a long way toward happiness and a good relationship.

Money Spending Conflicts

Money spending conflicts center around either overspending or spending more money on something than your partner thinks you should have. Once the money is spent, there are few things that can be done except to return the purchase (if possible), or prevent future expenditures. Most arguments about overspending are a poor attempt to change a partner's spending habits. That is to say, argument is used as punishment so that the partner won't spend foolishly in the future. I never recommend the use of punishment in relationships, but people use it because it works *a little*. It has very harmful side effects, however.

Criticism as punishment

Punishment, to be effective, has to be severe and consistent. Mild punishment (short-lived complaining), and infrequent punishment (occasional complaining) results in people either getting used to the punishment or gambling that the punishment won't happen ("maybe he won't be upset this time"). Mild punishment cannot compete with an emotional need when it comes to changing behavior. People will simply put up with criticism to continue to do what they want.

Criticism or other punishment would have to be severe to be effective. But, severe punishment damages relationships severely. It creates an imbalance, with one partner acting in the parental role, or worse yet, in an abusive role. If you are arguing about your partner's spending habits, you will have to weigh the helpfulness of the arguing against the damage that it is doing to your relationship. It's likely that either your arguing is ineffective because it is mild and inconsistent, or it is damaging your relationship because it is severe. In my work with thousands of people in relationships, I have yet to find a relationship where arguing and criticism actually were helpful. Can you imagine someone saying:

> *"Thanks to arguing, we solved our financial problems and improved our relationship."*

Or

> *"Thanks to my spouse's criticism, I became good at managing money and our relationship became close."*

If you have the fantasy that your situation will somehow improve by being critical or by complaining, it is time to give it up as unrealistic.

Secret spending

A problem related to arguing about spending is secret spending. Secret spending occurs because of fear of a partner's reaction should they find out either: 1) what the money is being spent on, 2) how much money is being spent, or 3) both. If the money is being spent on an addiction (including alcohol, drugs, or gambling) or an affair, that problem should be dealt with first rather than treating it as a financial issue. You may need to put boundaries around the access and use of money, but only within the context of dealing with the addiction or affair.

Secret spending does not always indicate that the person who is secretly spending is in the wrong. Sometimes it indicates that the other partner is overly controlling or unreasonable. In either case, secrecy is like a poison to the relationship—it may not take effect immediately, but after it builds up to a certain level, the relationship becomes very sick and may never recover.

If your spouse is not allowing you to spend money on what you reasonably need to survive, or your children reasonably need to survive, treat that as abuse. Don't fall for any reasoning that since you don't earn the money you shouldn't have any say in how it is spent. That would be like saying that because you are the one who vacuums the carpet, your spouse shouldn't be allowed to walk on it. Or because you cook the food, your spouse shouldn't be allowed to eat any of it. If you have to divorce (and I hope you never have to), you will find that the courts consider half of everything to be yours regardless of who paid for it (unless it was paid for before your marriage).

Financial selfishness

What do you do then, when your spouse is spending money which was budgeted for something else, or your spouse is spending most of the available fun money on his or her own fun, giving you little to spend on yourself? Once again, agreement and boundaries do a better job than arguing. Agreement will get you both to the place where you can talk about spending in a productive way. Boundaries will make sure that you don't continue to play a victim role. Combine agreement and boundaries with messages of love, and you are much more likely to end up being happier with your spouse, even when you both have to go through temporary financial hardship.

Tax Payment and Loan Repayment Conflicts

Here we get into issues of honesty, credit rating, and legality. Problems with these put you in danger of losing integrity, future buying power, future penalty, and possible jail time. All of these not only make your life more stressful, they also will leach the joy out of your marriage. In addition, if your spouse is doing something dishonest or illegal, you will lose respect for him or her.

The method of agreement can be used in such situations for agreeing on how difficult it is to pay interest or taxes, or even how it seems unfair. But, be careful not to agree to participate in fraud. Do not lend your signature, do not provide false information, and be very clear with your spouse that you will report him or her if he or she forges your signature. Some people are in relationships for the explicit purpose of defrauding their partner as well as creditors.

If your spouse becomes upset because of your refusal to participate in fraud or to borrow beyond your means to repay, then deal with it just as if your spouse was upset that you would not pay for his or her cocaine habit. That is, don't let the anger coerce you into being codependent for the behavior—it would result in nothing but harm for yourself and the relationship. The only thing codependence does is to avoid conflict for today, but today will be over in less than 24 hours.

Conflicts Over Buying Decisions

What happens when an impulse shopper marries a careful spender? Well, the impulse shopper uses up available funds secretly while the careful spender thinks about what to get, when to get it, what is the best price, and what is the best time to buy; or the impulse shopper becomes tired and frustrated with all the time and work put into making even small purchases. Some people will spend dollars more on gas just to drive across town where the chewing gum is cheaper.

Unless the budget is being overspent, this is not an issue of right and wrong and one style is not better than the other. Finding a way to make buying decisions *together* is the important issue. Fortunately, the method of agreement works well for this. Once a way of making such decisions is worked out, it does not need to continue to be a problem in the relationship.

If the budget is being overspent, then the conflict over buying decisions is actually an issue about spending. Think of it this way—if you have a lot of money, it hardly matters whether you can save a few dollars shopping around. But, if you have to break your piggy bank just to buy new socks, then it matters very much whether you can save money or not. *Spending conflicts* are caused by overspending available funds. *Buying conflicts* occur when there are enough funds, but the when, where, how, and why of spending causes problems.

Financial Problem or Communication Problem?

Just as a reminder, throughout this book I am showing you how to use agreement as a method to get to problem solving and a closer relationship. Perhaps there is no situation that so much demands this kind of approach as financial conflict, because financial conflict contributes so heavily to breakup and divorce. Except when one spouse is mainly concerned about receiving money in exchange for being in the relationship, conflicts *about* money cause more harm than actual financial problems. Proper money management is important, but so is the ability to work cooperatively.

Learning to manage money

People who try to solve their relationship problems solely by learning money management have the most success if both partners learn how to manage money together. This is because they learn a common language about money, discuss money in a context separate from other relationship issues, and come up with common goals about what they want to achieve with their money. When only one partner learns money management, it is far less likely to be helpful. Without a common language and knowledge base, there has to be sufficient trust in the relationship for one partner to leave the money management decisions to the other. When there is sufficient trust, there is nothing wrong with one person being in charge of the financial decisions. When there is not enough trust, either the trust must be earned or both partners need to get on the same page with money management principles. Which one is easier to do depends on the relationship.

If you can't learn money management together

If it is not possible for both partners to learn money management together, it can be very helpful for at least one partner to learn ways to improve *communication*. The method of agreement and the problem solving technique taught in this book are two good ways of improving communication. Positive communication improves cooperation and understanding.

Couples who communicate well are more open to learning and trying new things. So, if you have a resistant or controlling spouse, focusing on improving the communication between the both of you will then make it easier to deal with financial problems. If the communication is not in place, efforts to fix financial problems may just increase conflict. Improve communication first, then deal with financial problems. I have found that my clients can typically improve their communication enough in two weeks, using methods like the ones in this book, to begin working on financial problems.

Use Agreement to End Financial Conflicts

People have an intuitive feeling that talking about differences will lead to change, while agreement will lead to worsening problems. This is one case in which intuition fails us. Actually, talking about differences often leads to conflict, which then delays or prevents change. Agreement improves cooperation and makes change happen more quickly and easily. In this section, I will show you some ways to use agreement for each of the kinds of financial conflict discussed earlier.

Example: Typical low income conflict
SPOUSE 1: "We don't have enough money to pay all of our bills, and we are getting behind on car payments."

SPOUSE 2: "I know, I know. I am doing the best that I can. I am working my butt off as it is."

SPOUSE 1: "I'm not saying you need to do more."

SPOUSE 2: "What then? You are just trying to tell me that I'm a lousy provider? Maybe

*if you didn't spend so much money we would
have enough. Did you ever think of that?"*
*SPOUSE 1: "Look, I'm not trying to argue.
I'm just saying we have a problem."*
*SPOUSE 2: "Well, unless you can do
something about it, I don't want to hear
about it. I'm tired of you complaining all the
time about money. Do something about it or
leave me alone. I'm doing the best I can.
Case closed!"*
SPOUSE 1: [Retreats in silence]

What is evident in this dialogue is the highly charged emotions and feelings of inadequacy Spouse 2 has when money problems are brought up. Although not accused of anything, he or she rapidly becomes defensive and then attacking. Spouse 2 avoids Spouse 1 as a way of dealing with feelings of guilt and inadequacy. Spouse 1 will become more and more frustrated because money doesn't stretch and because he or she doesn't feel any *emotional* support in paying the bills. The end result will be two lonely people, both needing emotional support, but unable to give it to each other. And of course, the financial problems just add to the distress.

Let's take the same circumstances as this example, but have Spouse 1 use agreement rather than explanation.

Example: Handling low income conflict using the method of agreement (combined with problem solving)

*SPOUSE 1: "We don't have enough money
to pay all of our bills, and we are getting
behind on car payments."*
*SPOUSE 2: "I know, I know. I am doing the
best that I can. I am working my butt off as
it is."*

> *SPOUSE 1: "You sure are. I wish you didn't have to work so hard, but I really appreciate it."*
> *SPOUSE 2: "Even though I do the best I can, it's just not enough."*
> *SPOUSE 1: "I know. And I don't want you to work any harder than you do."*
> *SPOUSE 2: "But, we have to pay those damn bills. I hate them!"*
> *SPOUSE 1: "Me too. Nasty buggers."*
> *SPOUSE 2: "So, what am I supposed to do?"*
> *SPOUSE 1: "Well, I think you are supposed to sit down with me, so we can figure out some ways to make things a little easier. Maybe there are some ways I can help."*
> *SPOUSE 1: "Ok, I guess so."*
> *SPOUSE 2: "Here, come sit next to me. Let's get this problem down on paper and then go from there [shifts into problem solving].*

In this example, Spouse 2 gets defensive, but Spouse 1 does not try to explain that it wasn't an attack. Spouse 1 simply agrees with the defense. Even if Spouse 1 thinks that Spouse 2 will need to work more, possibly do overtime or get an additional job, the beginning of communication is *not* the time for solutions. Those can come out as brainstorm options during problem solving. The first step is not brainstorming solutions, but to reach agreement on the problem. After that, you can brainstorm together. Brainstorming sure couldn't be initiated with the typical conflict example given previously, because there was no agreement—just argument. Argument prevents agreement and problem solving.

As usual, I will assume that you are thinking that it really isn't that easy. You have had plenty of conflict about money before and you know that you can't just do a little agreement and shift into problem solving right away. Well, I couldn't agree with you more. If you have a history of conflict over this issue, then this example illustrates a goal you are trying to reach. It may take several conversations of agreeing before your spouse is willing to go through the problem solving steps with you. Let's take a look at how one of these preliminary discussions might go.

Example: Handling low income conflict using the method of agreement (with no problem solving)

SPOUSE 1: *"We don't have enough money to pay all of our bills, and we are getting behind on car payments."*

SPOUSE 2: *"I know, I know. I am doing the best that I can. I am working my butt off as it is."*

SPOUSE 1: *"You sure are. I wish you didn't have to work so hard, but I really appreciate it."*

SPOUSE 2: *"Even though I do the best I can, it's just not enough."*

SPOUSE 1: *"I know. And I don't want you to work any harder than you do."*

SPOUSE 2: *"But, we have to pay those damn bills. I hate them!"*

SPOUSE 1: *"Me too. Nasty buggers."*

SPOUSE 2: *"I don't want to talk about this anymore.'*

SPOUSE 1: *"Good idea. Let's get a cup of coffee (go for a walk, watch some TV, thumb wrestle, have sex, etc.)."*

What you can see in this example is that you don't have to get to problem solving immediately. This is especially true if you don't wait for problems to become crises before you start to work on them. Usually after having this kind of brief discussion a few times, your spouse will either come up with some possible answers, including your changing the way you do something, or else ask what you think should be done. In either case, don't focus on the idea your partner has, or lack of ideas, but use that to initiate the problem solving. If you are feeling blamed unjustly, the truth of the matter will become apparent to your spouse during the evaluation stage of the problem solving (be sure you have read the chapter on problem solving if you don't know what I am talking about).

Money saving and investing differences and the method of agreement

What if your spouse is resistant to meeting with a financial planner or even working on a budget with you? Is it time to start arguing and fighting to press the point home? Or is it time to avoid the issue altogether and let some future financial problem make the point for you? I suggest that you use the method of agreement to motivate your spouse to want to work on a budget and to plan for the future. That means appealing to the interests of your spouse. Some people fear that appealing to a partner's interests means giving up one's own interests. Nothing could be further from the truth. It is working against your partner's interests which will make him or her resist and fight yours. Let's take a look at both ways of talking.

Example: Traditional approach to handling saving/investing differences

SPOUSE 1: *"I've been thinking we really should put some money away for emergencies and for our retirement."*
SPOUSE 2: *"Makes sense."*
SPOUSE 1: *"We can put some money in a bank account for emergencies and some in long term mutual funds for our retirement."*
SPOUSE 2: *"How much money are you talking about?"*

SPOUSE 1: "Well, if we live in a smaller house and stop replacing our cars every three years, we can save a lot."

SPOUSE 2: "I'm not going to drive around in a clunker for 10 years and stay trapped in a small house until I'm in my 60's."

SPOUSE 1: "Well, it's either that or cut down on our living expenses."

SPOUSE 2: "So, you want me to get my clothes at lawn sales and give up my activities with my friends? I don't think so."

SPOUSE 1: "We have to take the money from somewhere."

SPOUSE 2: "Well take it from your own expenses. My activities are important. I work hard. You can't expect me to give up my lifestyle just so you can live it up when you are old."

SPOUSE 1: "The money is for US. Why should I give up my lifestyle, while you maintain your lifestyle? Look, I'm trying to help you and you are acting like I'm trying to hurt you."

SPOUSE 2: "Wanting me to live in a small house, drive an old car, and give up my activities doesn't sound very helpful to me...."

This conversation is typical in that spouses will agree on having savings and a nice retirement fund, but are most likely to resist when it means giving up something they value right now. They then start defending and attacking, which serves to derail the communication about saving/investing. In this situation, every solution you come up with will be rejected because saving for the future means either earning more money or spending less in the present. Neither of these is appealing, especially if you already have a strained relationship and your spouse is doubtful about the future of your relationship. Let's tweak the above example using the method of agreement.

Example: Saving/investing differences and the method of agreement.

SPOUSE 1: "I've been thinking we really should put some money away for emergencies and for our retirement."

SPOUSE 2: "Makes sense."

Spouse1: "What would you like our life to be like when we retire? I mean, where would you like to live and what kinds of things would you like to do for fun?"

SPOUSE 2: "I think I'd really like to live near the beach."

SPOUSE 1: "That sounds beautiful. Let's put our heads together and see how we could work on making that a reality for us."

SPOUSE 2: "How do we do that?"

SPOUSE 1: "Well, we don't need to make any decisions right away. Let's just make some notes and talk about some ideas for getting what we really want at retirement."

SPOUSE 2: "Ok, I guess."

Spouse 1: "Let's go out for a coffee while we talk about it."

SPOUSE 2: "Sounds good."

The major difference between this way and the traditional way, in the previous example, is that with this way there are no immediate suggestions or solutions. There really is little that your spouse can find fault with since you are in agreement with whatever he or she said was desirable for the future. What if you don't want to live next to the ocean (as in this example)? It makes no difference. Planning to be able to do so will allow you to talk about saving and investing just the same as if you were talking about being able to live in the mountains. Who knows, by the time you retire, you may like the beach or your spouse may not. At least you will have some choices with a good retirement fund. If you always focus on the priorities, the other stuff will take care of itself.

Another difference with this method is that Spouse 1 doesn't present any ideas or solutions for investing. The time for that will be after they start problem solving. If you remember, in the problem solving process it's desirable to talk about both positive and negative aspects of all ideas and to weigh these ideas against each other. Doing that, your spouse is much more likely to come to agreement with you (or you with him or her) than if you initially present your own ideas and argue about them.

One more point about this example is that the conversation shifted away from emergency saving to retirement only. That is fine. There is no need to do everything all at once. You will get more done if you work on one thing at a time.

Use Agreement to Make a Budget

Budgets are marriage savers. They put both spouses on the same page and create spending limits that both spouse's agree on. They help people to get out of debt, and they also create a "fun money" allowance fund for each partner so that they don't need to feel guilty or ask "permission" before spending money on themselves.

My wife and I started using the envelope system early in our marriage, and we still use it today. We have a set of envelopes, one for each monthly expense category (food, clothes, medicine, insurance, taxes, donations, etc.) as well annual expense categories (insurance, taxes, licenses, professional training, kids' tuition, etc.), fun money (dating, my allowance, my wife's allowance), and emergency savings. We have calculated how much we need to put in each envelope, each month. If more money is needed than is available in an envelope, it is taken from another envelope. Although this is a simple system, it keeps us out of debt, makes sure we always have money for our bills, gives us money for dating and travel, and gives us personal money we can do whatever we want with. If you would like to use "the envelope system," you can learn more about it online or from books. It's been around a long time.

Let's take a look at a couple of ways you might talk to your spouse about making a budget.

Example: Talking about making a budget (traditional way)

SPOUSE 1: "I think we need to make a budget. We are way overspending in some areas and getting into more and more debt."

SPOUSE 2: "We don't have any money to make a budget with. And, I'm already careful with my spending."

SPOUSE 1: "I think we both could handle our money better and maybe cut out some luxuries."

SPOUSE 2: "What luxuries? You call getting new vacuum cleaner bags a luxury?"

SPOUSE 1: "No, of course not, but we are making too much debt."

SPOUSE 2: "Well, you make a budget if you want to, but leave me out. I don't need you controlling the way I spend money when I'm already careful."

The real purpose of a budget is to allow people to continue to do what is most important to them, but most people think of a budget like going on a diet. It's usually not a good idea to present a budget as a way to cut down on spending.

Here is another way you can talk about a budget that has more of a partnership feel, and less of a professor know-it-all feel.

Example: Using the method of agreement to talk about a budget

SPOUSE 1: "You and I both have things we like to do and buy, but I'm concerned that our debt is going to make that more and more difficult for us."

SPOUSE 2: "It can't be helped. We are doing everything we can."

SPOUSE 1: "It does seem that way, doesn't it."

SPOUSE 2: "We both work, we don't spend money on foolish things, and the things we have debt for would be hard to live without. We can't get to work without cars and we have to live somewhere."

SPOUSE 1: "Isn't that the truth. I guess it would help me to feel more in control if I could see where our money is going. Would you sit down with me and go through that with me?"

SPOUSE 2: "We can, but it's not going to make any difference."

SPOUSE 1: "You may be right, but I really appreciate you doing it with me."

SPOUSE 2: "Whatever."

In this example, Spouse 2 is not thrilled about going over expenses with Spouse 1. Honestly, it's not a thrilling process. But, it's a great start to getting them both on the same page. The figures will make the point for Spouse 1, without him or her having to work on convincing.

The only time figures won't convince your spouse is if you are wrong. And, if you are wrong, that's good to find out too. Either way, it results in you and your spouse getting on the same page about your financial situation. Then you will be in the position to work on solutions using the method of problem solving. Financial problems require real solutions and can't be argued away or indefinitely avoided.

Contrary to popular belief, a budget is *essential* for people who do not have enough money to pay their bills. Budgeting helps people to get out of debt. And, budgeting helps them to have more of what they want—not less. Use the truth of this to appeal to your spouse's interests.

Example: Traditional approach to money spending differences

> SPOUSE 1: *"I think it's time to get a new car. Ours is starting to break down and we need a bigger one now that we have two kids."*
>
> SPOUSE 2: *"Yeah, we have two kids—that's why we can't afford a new car."*
>
> SPOUSE 1: *"That's it! You just decide what I can and can't have. There's no discussion. I just have to follow you, and I'm sick of it."*
>
> SPOUSE 2: *"What is there to discuss? I can't pull money out of a hat. Do you want to get another job and take care of the kids at the same time? Can YOU do that?"*

In this example, Spouse 1 and 2 may both be right. It really might be time for a bigger car, even if it isn't a new one. And, there may be no money currently available for purchasing a car. These are objective facts, but they can't discuss them because the discussion has turned into an emotional argument about control. This type of interaction does a lot of harm to a relationship. Spouse 2 may be right, but hammering his or her spouse with the facts creates anger and frustration, which push them apart.

Example: Using agreement with money spending differences

> SPOUSE 1: *"I think it's time to get a new car. Ours is starting to break down and we need a bigger one now that we have two kids."*
>
> SPOUSE 2: *"A new car sure would be nice, wouldn't it. I wonder if we can afford it, though."*
>
> SPOUSE 1: *"I don't think we can afford to keep putting money into the one we have. It's only going to get worse, not better. And, it might become unsafe for the kids."*
>
> SPOUSE 2: *"Those are really good points. I hadn't considered that. Let's sit down and go over some ideas. Maybe getting a new car will turn out to be the best one."*

In this example, Spouse 2 has set the stage for problem solving by being agreeable rather than disagreeable. It isn't necessary to immediately shoot down Spouse 1's idea. That would just close down communication and damage the relationship. Instead, during the problem solving, they can both go over the costs and benefits of getting a new car. They can also consider other ideas.

The main point is that although Spouse 2 may have an immediate internal reaction that getting a new car is a bad idea or not possible, he or she does not immediately try to convince his or her spouse of that. Instead, he or she agrees that it *may* be a good idea, helping his or her spouse feel supported. Trust in the problem solving process rather than in trying to convince your spouse through argument, force of will or intellect. If your spouse wants something and you use force of will, you will be attempting to control or overpower your spouse. If you attempt to shut down your spouse by being smart, it will only make him or her feel dumb. Making your spouse feel dumb is not a smart thing to do. Problem solving let's you guide rather than control. And, who knows, maybe you will both come up with an even better idea.

Troubleshooting

"I can't find anything to agree with about my spouse's ideas."

You have probably gotten used to the idea that there are right solutions and wrong solutions and this is interfering with your ability to consider positive aspects of what your spouse is saying. *Everything* has both good and bad aspects. To take an extreme example, let's say that your spouse says, "I want to use all of our bill money to buy drugs." While we know that is a very bad idea, it is not without some positive aspects as well. For example, buying drugs may be exciting, or help your spouse to forget his or her problems for a while. By agreeing with these aspects, you are making a connection with your spouse, which will help him or her to also consider other aspects of buying drugs as well as other ideas. When all the aspects are considered, your spouse is likely to reject his or her own idea.

Counselors have been using this method for decades to connect with their clients. Instead of getting freaked out when their client comes up with a terrible idea, the counselor asks how it would help and then agrees with those things. Connection made, the client then is more open to hearing the therapist's ideas. If the therapist simply said, "That's crazy!" the client would walk out the door and never come back. Therapists know that to really help clients make good decisions, they need to maintain a good relationship with them. That is true in your marriage as well. Consider your partner's ideas first if you want him or her to consider yours.

"We made a budget, but my spouse won't follow it."

This is the reason that the problem solving method, introduced in this book, includes making a backup plan each and every time you and your spouse decide on a solution. Having a backup plan encourages people to stick with the first plan, and also gives them recourse if the first plan is not working. Your backup plan for this situation could have been any of a number of different possibilities such as having a third party manage the bills and give you both allowances, attending a support group for over spenders, getting financial coaching, attending marital counseling, or even having a marital separation if the situation was severe enough.

These ideas would likely be less desirable to your spouse and would have helped him or her to maintain the budget. And, they would give you something to do now rather than to feel stuck. At this point, you can try to restart the problem solving and make new plans—including a backup plan. If that fails, the main problem has become one of communication and relationship, with a financial problem only being a side effect of that. If communication is not possible, I recommend relationship coaching to help you get the communication restarted.

How can relationship coaching help with a financial problem?

If your relationship is otherwise good, and your problem is limited to finances, then getting financial counseling makes more sense than relationship coaching. However many people with financial problems have many conflicts and difficulty communicating well enough to make progress on their finances. They also may not be able to come to agreement about getting financial counseling. Without some repair and strengthening of the relationship, the relationship could fail. Financial problems would be a contributor to such a breakup or divorce, but an inability to work together on the financial problems would be the biggest contributor.

Summary

Arguing about financial problems damages relationships without solving financial problems. The method of agreement improves relationships while providing a positive way to talk about financial solutions. The method of agreement is not used to blindly accept your spouse's ideas, but rather to keep communication positive so you can discuss various ideas. The first step is agreeing that your spouse has some good points and that his or her ideas should be considered along with other possible solutions. There are thus two stages of dealing with financial problems: 1) being open and agreeable, and 2) transitioning to problem solving. If this is done before making financial changes, there will be more cooperation as well as a backup plan—resulting in an improved relationship as well as improved finances.

Doubt that the stars are fire;
Doubt that the sun doth move;
Doubt truth to be a liar;
But never doubt I love.

William Shakespeare
from *Hamlet*

♥12♥

USING AGREEMENT WHEN YOUR SPOUSE HAS A PSYCHOLOGICAL DISORDER

There is a good chance that either you or your spouse will suffer from a psychological disorder for at least a portion of your marriage. Although you can find a lot of information on the treatment of mental disorders, there is much less information on how to help a spouse with a psychological disorder. There is even less information on how to improve your marriage when your spouse has a psychological disorder. Fortunately, the method of agreement can be applied here, as well.

According to the National Institute of Mental Health, each year about one fourth of US adults suffer from a diagnosable mental disorder and many from more than one.[3] Many psychological disorders are both mild and temporary and can result from sudden or gradual changes in living conditions. Other disorders are more severe and can result from trauma in childhood or as an adult. Some psychological disorders also have a strong genetic or

---

[3] National Institute of Mental Health. *The Numbers Count: Mental Disorders in America*. Retrieved from NIMH website: http://www.nimh.nih.gov/health/publications/the-numbers-count-mental-disorders-in-america/index.shtml on November 28, 2012.

biological component. All psychological disorders have one thing in common—they make normal functioning difficult. This includes functioning in relationships.

Psychological Disorders and Relationships

There are many kinds of psychological disorders. The most common psychological disorders are mood disorders (e.g. depression and bipolar disorders), anxiety disorders (e.g. generalized anxiety disorder and panic disorder), and adjustment disorders. Regardless of the type of disorder, it is likely to result in increased stress within your relationship. The more changes that result from the psychological disorder, and it's treatment, the more stress will be placed on your relationship. If the disorder is mild or temporary, the stress may also be mild or temporary.

Sometimes though, there is enough stress caused as a result of a disorder that it threatens a relationship. When it does, the obvious step is getting psychological help for the person with the disorder, but that step is often insufficient. His or her partner needs help, too. It's all well and good to say, "My husband (or wife) is in counseling for his problem, so I just have to be patient." It's quite another thing to know how to maintain the relationship while you are being patient. This is especially true if the psychological disorder is chronic or cycling. People make a commitment to stay together, "for better, for worse; in sickness and in health." Even so, people have limits of what they can do and what they can take. Most of us are not born saints, nor are we close to becoming one.

In my experience, anxiety disorders often create insecurity and neediness which imbalance relationships. As a result, one partner becomes more like a parent. Depressions often "weigh down" relationships and take the fun out of them. As a result, the grass starts looking a lot greener with other partners. Even if such desires are not acted on, they increase the dissatisfaction with one's own partner. Like it or not, these are part of the realities of being a human being. Working on our marriage, and these issues in particular, will work better in the long run than trying to be patient.

When a Psychological Disorder Becomes an Excuse

A potential problem is that when a spouse is diagnosed with a psychological disorder, all of the problems in the relationship often are blamed on the disorder. It too often becomes an explanation or excuse for behaviors which are really damaging to the relationship, but may not be a direct result of the disorder. When the disorder is used as an excuse for harmful behaviors, both spouses become a victim of the disorder.

As a marriage and relationship coach, I teach people that someone else can make you a victim, but if you are repeatedly being victimized, you must somehow be allowing it to happen. This doesn't change just because your spouse has a psychological disorder. However, spouses of partners with mental disorders often feel guilty or mean if they takes a stand against emotional or physical abuse. They allow themselves to be mistreated because their partner "can't help it." Aside from psychotic disorders though, psychological disorders do not cause a person to be abusive. Even if your spouse had a psychotic disorder, it would still be necessary to put limits in place which would prevent the abuse from recurring. It never helps anyone to allow abuse to continue. Even if you consider such abuse "accidental," you still need to protect yourself from it.

Spouses who use their disorder as an excuse may complain about their partner's lack of understanding and sympathy. This can increase their partner's feelings of guilt, anger, anxiety, depression, or any combination thereof. Improperly managing a relationship with a person with a psychological disorder can result in your own psychological disorder.

People with disorders can also become self-condemning in a way which only makes their condition worse (e.g. "Because I'm so depressed, I'm no good to anybody and I can't do anything"). They may be so focused on their problems that they don't think about the effect of their problems on their spouse or children. Disorder or not, that is still selfishness. Having a psychological disorder does not remove our responsibility to show loving kindness to those we are committed to.

213

The Healthy Partner Can Remove the Excuse

It may seem crazy, but the person who has the most power to help both herself (or himself) and her spouse is the one *without* the psychological disorder. The healthier a person is, the easier it is to make changes. Family therapists know that if you have a child with a behavior problem, you don't fix the child. You help the parents know how to better deal with the behavior. Then, the child improves.

For years, I've been working with men and women who have partners with some real problems. Instead of encouraging them to divorce, I teach them how to change the outcome of what their spouse does. If you control the outcome, you control the behavior. In this chapter, it is my intention to teach you how to use both the method of agreement and boundaries, for the purpose of improving your relationship. The fact that your spouse has a psychological disorder in no way means that your relationship can't grow.

This information is often not to be found in relationship self-help books. Some therapists will scoff and say that I have said too little because I have not gone into detail about the nature of the psychological disorders nor considered all the nuances associated with them. What I hope you see instead is that rather than saying, "I can't help you," I am offering what I know, although I agree it is insufficient. While I'm not giving you all the pieces to the puzzle, I am giving you a significant piece of it. There are other pieces available elsewhere.

If the piece I contribute helps you to have a little bit better relationship, then I will have at least done something where many have done nothing. I do not want to be like the stingy man who was asked for some money by a hungry beggar and reply, "Sorry, I can't help you. I only have 25 cents and that won't be much use to you. Why don't you ask someone else?" Instead, I will give you my 25 cents worth and also encourage you to collect nickels, dimes, and quarters from others until you have what you need. There are many resources available on specific disorders. One of

214

the best sources of information online is the National Institute of Mental Health.[4]

Three Typical Relationship Problems

The following are a few of the ways that communication can deteriorate when one spouse has a mental illness. You will see that with all three of these ways of communication, the main problem is a loss of equality and partnership. Emotional closeness and cooperation are sacrificed to accommodate the effects of the psychological disorder. An additional sacrifice is the happiness of the spouse who does not have the disorder (the secondary victim). With emotional closeness gone and happiness gone, the only thing left is duty/obligation/responsibility. These are not bad qualities, but they can lead to burnout. If you get burned out helping your spouse, *you* will be the one needing the most help.

Becoming a martyr/servant/nurse

What can happen sometimes is that we can fall into the role of *primarily* taking care of our partner. This has the effect of lowering our status and raising our spouse's. The hope is (at least initially) that the psychological disorder will run its course and only be temporary, much like if it was the flu. The servant-spouse focuses on being patient and pleasing—no matter how ridiculous or abusive the partner's behavior.

> **SPOUSE WITH DISORDER: "I can't go out with you. Don't you get it? I am depressed. That means I don't feel like doing anything. So get off my back about going out with you."**

---

[4] The National Institute of Mental Health (NIMH) is part of The National Institutes of Health (NIH), a component of the U.S. Department of Health and Human Services. You can find them on the web at: http://www.nimh.nih.gov.

> *SERVANT SPOUSE: "I'm sorry. I didn't mean to upset you."*
> *SPOUSE WITH DISORDER: "I would think by now you would have learned. Just don't bug me anymore."*
> *SERVANT SPOUSE: "Ok, ok. I will stay right here and take care of you. "*
> *SPOUSE WITH DISORDER: "I should hope so. I didn't ask to have this problem, you know."*

In this example, the disorder is depression, but you could easily substitute any other disorder. I don't know about you, but my level of patience for my own mistreatment is very low (with people who can control their behavior, that is). I could put up with this kind of behavior for about a day...maybe. Yet, incredibly there are many people who are replaying this scenario over and over and blaming themselves if they become impatient.

The sad thing is that the sacrifices of the servant-spouse do not actually aid his or her spouse in recovery. If anything, they may add extra incentive for the spouse *not* to recover. The main problem is failing to distinguish between the psychological *symptoms*, which are beyond the partner's control, and the *behaviors* which are not a direct result of the disorder. In our example above, the servant-spouse is losing respect very quickly. The spouse with the disorder has gained some kind of authoritarian status by virtue of having a disorder. But, mental disorders do not qualify people to be in authority.

In this example, one spouse has depression. With depression it is true that people will not feel like making an effort to go out. This is a *symptom* of depression. But, rudeness, inconsideration, and emotional abusiveness are not symptoms of depression. They are the *behaviors* you need to deal with. We can't demand that our spouses feel happy and energetic, but we can demand to be treated with respect. If you observe carefully, people with psychological disorders may talk nicely to their friends or doctors and rudely to their spouses. What does this tell you? That they have control over their behavior. There is a definite choice being made here.

Even an irritable or angry person has no right to be an abusive person. Allowing such abusiveness is not part of being a good spouse. It is part of codependence.

Sometimes, this kind of behavior happens with well meaning parents who feel sorry for their child. When I worked with the Association for Retarded Citizens (ARC-San Diego), I got to see many developmentally delayed children and adults who had been allowed by their parents to have all sorts of behaviors that made it more difficult for them to be able to be in public. They needed to be trained, and their parents needed to be trained how to set limits and disallow harmful behaviors in order to improve the functioning of their children. They needed to regain their parenting role and to stop just being caretakers. Spouses also have to make sure that they are continuing to be spouses and not just caretakers.

My opinion is if someone is dying, be as patient as you can, but stay safe; if someone is not dying, then do whatever you can to help them live better. Sometimes that may mean that you are nice, but often it may mean that you set healthy boundaries, and make sure you are not codependent for their problems. Just as we don't buy alcohol for an alcoholic (substance abuse disorder), we don't sit at home with our depressed spouse, continually reassure our overanxious spouse, or tolerate verbal or physical abuse from our stressed spouse (impulse control disorder). To do so wouldn't be doing them or ourselves any favors.

Becoming a doctor/mother/father to your spouse

The servant role puts the spouse with the disorder in a higher position. The doctor/mother/father role puts the spouse with the disorder in a *lower* position. Control is maintained by the healthy spouse who supposedly "knows better." Some people with disorders easily fall into the submissive role and welcome their spouse to be their parental caretaker. It absolves them of responsibility for making decisions and having to think.

This kind of relationship can be remarkably stable for a long time, but eventually becomes tiresome for either partner. When the spouse without the disorder recovers, it can make the caretaker spouse feel less needed, and less important. This can bring about relapse or an end of the relationship. Codependency in this situation also prolongs the psychological disorder.

If you are the partner with the disorder, and your spouse is controlling your every move and decision, you need to determine if he or she is really helping you or is mainly providing an excuse for you to stay sick. Don't mistake feeling better with getting better. Some things that make us feel better maintain our problems. Would you have already recovered without your spouse's help? Is it too easy to be "sick"? Be aware of the treatment for your disorder so you can know if your spouse is really helping or keeping you dependent.

Example unhelpful control by a caretaking spouse:

YOU: "I think I would like to try going for a walk around the block. It's been a while since I have been out of the house."

SPOUSE: "That's true, but what if you get another panic attack? Do you remember what happened two years ago when you had a panic attack at the department store? Do you really want to go through that again?"

YOU: "No, I guess not. It was just an idea."

SPOUSE: "Someday you can do such things. Right now, you need to just focus on taking your pills and getting better."

I remember a story I heard once about a couple who had a little preschool boy with metal leg braces. When they were leaving a restaurant the child fell in the parking lot and was struggling with trying to get up. His metal leg braces made it hard for him to get up. To the amazement of onlookers, the parents did not help their child to get up although he was continuing to struggle and having a difficult time. Finally, one of the onlookers asked the parents why they weren't helping their child to get up. The parents explained that although it was hard to see their son struggle, it would be even harder on their son if they didn't let him learn how to get up by himself. Eventually, the boy got up.

Just as we need to recognize the difference between being nice to someone and helping someone, we also need to recognize the difference in the treatment we receive from other people. Not everyone who is nice to us is really helping us. I choose the professionals I hire (doctors, mechanics, plumbers, financial advisors, etc.) based on how much they actually help me, even if they have the personality of a goat.

I don't have a reputation for being an overly nice coach. But, I do have a reputation for being a helpful, resourceful, and caring coach. Many times my clients do not have another person in their life who is both honest and caring. I can be tough when I need to be. One of the finest compliments that I have received is, "You don't always tell me what I want to hear, but you always help me." You can be this way for your spouse, and you can help your spouse to be this way for you. When a person is truly helping, they won't always be nice. Remember the couple who had the little boy with leg braces? They were being helpful, because at that moment it was more important than being nice.

Avoidance

Long term avoidance causes a gradual deterioration in relationships. In the short term, however, it is not a bad strategy. It may even be necessary. For example, it may be necessary to separate and have no direct contact with an abusive spouse until he or she has received a certain amount of assistance. Even then, interaction should not be suddenly recommenced, but occur in stages—both to help you, as well as to help your spouse.

Although I am not an advocate of divorce, I recognize that it is sometimes necessary to divorce from someone who has a chronic condition that is beyond our ability to deal with. The realities of life are that we have a responsibility to do all that we can to love others, but we all have limits beyond which we can do no more. When that limit is reached, walking away may become the best alternative. There have been many who, rather than walking away, killed themselves or their spouse. There have been many more who lived out their lives in quiet desperation. Would it have been better if they had walked away? Definitely.

The most common misuse of avoidance is to deal with a *chronic* problem. Avoidance is the easiest thing to do today, it will be the easiest thing to do tomorrow, but each day it eats away at a relationship like mold eats away at bread. The best way to stop using avoidance is to substitute effective actions that, although difficult today, will be a little easier tomorrow, and will cause your relationship to grow richer and deeper like a fine wine. As we will see a little later, the agreement method along with good boundaries is very effective for building good relationships, even with a spouse who has a psychological disorder.

Example of avoidance:
YOU: "Let's make love tonight. We haven't been together for a long time."
SPOUSE: "You know I just don't feel like it with my problem."
{as the months go by}
YOU: [say nothing about sex]
SPOUSE: [says nothing about sex]
[Sexless marriage results].

Some people marry because they believe they have found someone who will never reject them as others have, only to find themselves repeatedly rejected. One of the questions I routinely ask people at the start of our work is if they feel alone, even when they are with their partner. If they do, then I know that one or both of them is using avoidance.

Balance Agreement with Boundaries

To successfully avoid becoming a martyr, servant, doctor, parent, or roommate to your spouse, it is important to balance your own needs with those of your partner. If you take care of him or her at the expense of your own needs, eventually you will be drained of happiness, motivation, and all love for your partner. The same thing could happen with parents who don't balance their own needs with those of their children. They can find themselves resenting their children and wishing they never had them.

Do you know the emergency oxygen mask instructions for passengers on airplanes? The flight attendants tell you that if you are traveling with a child, to put on your own oxygen mask before helping your child with his or hers. The reason is quite simple. If you help your child with his or her oxygen mask before you put yours on, then you may become unconscious and unable to help your child, who also will not be able to help you put on your mask. Taking care of yourself first is vital to being able to take care of anyone else, whether spouse, partner, parent, or child.

Agreement is important, because it will help to maintain connection. Fighting certainly wouldn't be helpful. Also, agreeing will help you to feel better about the boundaries you need to set. Guilt is not a friend to relationships, so it is important that you feel good about what you are doing. You must always keep in mind that taking care of yourself is for the good of your relationship. It is also unrealistic to expect your spouse to agree with your boundaries, even if you explain them carefully and repeatedly. It is not important to convince your spouse of the importance of your boundaries. It is merely important to keep them.

Do Your Research First

Whether your spouse's condition is mental, physical, or both, it will be in your best interest to learn all you can about the disorder(s). There is a social component to all illnesses and disorders (e.g. when people have the flu, they are less interested in sex). What you will want to be able to do is to determine when you are being helpful and when you are being codependent. It is not codependent to stay home and take care of someone who has the flu. But, is it codependent to stay home and comfort someone who has an anxiety disorder? Usually the answer is yes.

Why is the same behavior codependent for one illness, but not for the other? Well, the person with the flu will benefit from your hands-on care. The person with the anxiety disorder will feel better, but will not benefit. More often an anxious person will benefit from a supportive spouse who will get them to stay engaged with the world—even if it makes them uncomfortable. Knowing more about the disorder and it's treatment will make you sure about the best way to help.

If you don't know about the disorder, it's symptoms, and treatment, you will be open to manipulation by your spouse and become unwittingly codependent. Researching the disorder will also help you to be an advocate for your spouse and will help to ensure that your spouse gets proper treatment from professionals. Your main goals in being a loving and helpful spouse are twofold: 1) to see that your spouse gets the best treatment possible; and 2) to maintain your relationship in a healthy way. It is the combination of these two things which will most help your partner and yourself, in the long run.

Use Agreement to Avoid Martyrdom

Your spouse can't make you a martyr without your help. Using the method of agreement, you can be helpful while avoiding becoming a martyr.

Example use of agreement and healthy boundaries with a mentally ill partner:
SPOUSE WITH DISORDER: "I can't go out with you. Don't you get it? I am depressed. That means I don't feel like doing anything. So get off my back about going out with you."
YOU: "I get it. Thank you for being clear with me. It is helpful to know. I will just leave the invitation open, but not keep

asking you. Instead, I will go out without you.
SPOUSE: "What? You are going out without me? Don't you think that is a little selfish for you to go out and have a good time while I'm miserable, all alone, at home?"
YOU: "Yes, I can see how it really feels that way to you. I wish you didn't need to feel miserable or be alone."
SPOUSE: "Then you will stay home."
YOU: "No, that would only make me burn out and that wouldn't help you."
SPOUSE: "Oh, that's all bullshit and you know it."
YOU: "I'm not going to argue with you."
SPOUSE: "Go then. I don't care!"

It is rare, but it sometimes happens that partners threaten suicide in the face of boundaries. The obvious reason is to get you to give up your boundaries, but it could also happen with spouses who have a history of suicidal behavior, or who are close to the limit of their ability to cope. While giving up your boundaries would harm your relationship, suicidal threats should always be taken seriously. In such a situation it is best to work with a qualified professional (such as a psychologist) to help you to have good boundaries while also maximizing your spouse's safety.

Most partners are not likely to become suicidal. They are more likely to be angry at first. Anger is an attempt to restore the status quo and is to be expected. The anger will gradually dissipate and over time they are likely to surprise you by wanting to go out with you, but don't expect that in the first couple of weeks. As with all changes you make, your spouse will persist until it is clear that your changes are permanent. Then, as much as it is difficult for your partner to get out, it will be more difficult to stay home alone. Getting out and socializing is very healthy behavior, regardless of how a person feels.

If you are ever in doubt about whether your boundaries are helpful or harmful, ask a counselor, coach, or someone who is an expert in treating the type of disorder your spouse has.

In the case of children or adults who need supervisory care, you will need to arrange for that before going out. Be sure that you make a habit of doing that though, or things will get worse.

If you are going to go to the trouble of sacrificing your happiness for your spouse, make sure it really is going to benefit him or her in the long run. Think through what will become of your relationship as you continue to do for your spouse whatever it is you are doing. If you already have been helping for some time, take a careful look at how it has affected your relationship. If it's getting worse, find a better way to help.

Avoiding Resentment

The general rule in care giving is not to regularly do something for people that they can do for themselves. It will just make them more dependent while making you feel resentful. If you are regularly doing something for your spouse that he or she could do, ask yourself why you are doing it. If it is out of love, then don't stop. But, if it is out of duty or obligation, take a look at what it could be doing to your love. You may be helping too much. If you feel yourself starting to resent doing something for your spouse, then you are either doing it too much, or for the wrong reasons. Use your resentment as a signal to either change what you are doing, to rethink why you are doing it, or to get professional help for your relationship. Resentment is a sign that you are on the way to emotional burnout and something needs to change.

Resentment is something *we* create, although we blame others for it. So, when we are resenting doing something for someone, we are really choosing to continue to do what makes us resentful. Since it is our choice, it is also our responsibility. We can take care of it by ourselves. The good news about that is that if we had to wait for someone else to fix our resentments, it might never happen. Because we can do it ourselves, things can improve rapidly.

Be a Partner, Not a Parent

What's wrong with being your spouse's doctor or caretaker? The main problem with it is that in order to be that, you have to sacrifice partnership. Partnership is only possible among equals.

In order to maintain a partnership with a person who has a mental illness or psychological disorder, it is important to distinguish between what is your responsibility and what is your spouse's responsibility. If your spouse is capable, you have to be careful not to repeatedly tell him or her what to do.

If your spouse has lost the ability to reason and remember, as with advanced Alzheimer's disease, then you are not going to have a partnership. Your role will necessarily become more parental. Even so, as much as you can, allow your partner to have as much choice and freedom as is safe for him or her.

I have high blood pressure. When I first started taking medication, I would sometimes forget whether I had already taken my pill. If I thought I forgot, I would take another one. If I thought I took it already, then I wouldn't. Sometimes this resulted in under-medicating myself and sometimes it would result in overmedicating myself. I hope you can tell by this book that I am not senile (if you can't, then maybe I am senile and don't know it!). How did my wife handle my forgetting about my medication? She gave me a pillbox divided into the days of the week. That was enough to keep me independent about my pills. Had she taken over the job of giving me my pill each morning, or asking me if I had taken it, she would have taken a step toward being my caretaker *when it was unnecessary.*

If you are caretaking, carefully assess where you might be caretaking unnecessarily and where you may also be controlling unnecessarily. People with a mental illness don't always do what is good for them. But, do you know what? People without a mental illness don't either. My wife is a weight conscious person, looks very nice, and I appreciate it. She knows high sugar, high fat foods are unhealthy. But, when she sees me walking home from the corner store eating an ice cream cone, she doesn't slap it out of my hand or give me a lecture on eating healthy. Nor does she remind me about my blood pressure. In her mind, the risk of the ice cream cone does not outweigh the benefit of a wonderful relationship. There is also the fact that she doesn't want the hassle of micromanaging me or wondering if I'm sneaking off for mint chocolate chip.

Be as educated as you can regarding your spouse's illness or disorder, and then draw a line between helping too much and helping too little, as best as you can.

> ### Example of agreement without control:
> **SPOUSE: "I think I would like to try going for a walk around the block. It's been a while since I have been out of the house."**
> **YOU: "That sounds like a good idea. Would you like me to walk with you?"**
> **SPOUSE: "No, that's ok. I think I would rather go by myself."**
> **YOU: "Ok, have a good walk."**

If you compare this with the example I gave earlier in the chapter, you can see how this example uses agreement whereas the previous example used control. Also, in this example, there is the offer of help, but there is no insistence. Yet a third difference is that in this example, you are knowledgeable about your spouse's disorder and can feel comfortable about your spouse's decision.

Agreement Stops Avoidance

Avoiders are going to avoid as long as their behavior works with you. They won't give up avoidance voluntarily or happily, but they will give it up if you use good boundaries. Their initial reluctance should be expected and allowed. Don't let it bother you that they don't want to change. No one wants to change. We all want others to change. Healthy people don't change because they want to, but because they think it is worth it in order to reach their goals. Unhealthy people don't try to change at all. You must light the fire and motivate them to change.

Example of using agreement and problem solving to help an avoidant spouse:

YOU: "Let's make love tonight. We haven't been together for a long time."

SPOUSE: "You know I just don't feel like it with my problem."

YOU: "Yes, I know you don't feel like it, and that people with your problem often don't feel like doing many things."

SPOUSE: "Well, that's the way it is."

YOU: "It sure is. And, I don't want to lose you over this issue. I'm sure that would cause even more problems for you, and I would miss you, too."

SPOUSE: "Are you saying that you are going to leave me if I don't have sex with you? "

YOU: "I'm just thinking that it could come to that eventually if we don't work on it."

SPOUSE: "Well, what do you expect me to do? Just become sexual on demand?"

YOU: "That might not work, but I think we could work together on some other options."

SPOUSE: "Like what?"

YOU: "Let's put our heads together and find something that is good for both of us."

[Getting out a piece of paper for problem solving]

SPOUSE: [Reluctantly complies]

No matter how difficult you think this would be to say and do with your spouse, I can tell you that it will be easier than having a sexless and emotionally distant marriage. If you have to sacrifice your relationship in order to maintain your marriage, you will eventually wonder "What's the point?" But, by then, you may be too burned out to do this kind of work and your spouse may care little about whether he or she loses you. Problems are best dealt with when they happen and while the relationship is still strong. This is true regardless of whether your spouse has a psychological disorder or not. This doesn't mean you need to run for a pencil and paper if your spouse has a headache one night. A pattern is something that happens more often than not.

Troubleshooting

Problems are not something to fear. They are something to expect and prepare for. That's why we keep a first aid kit in our home and a spare tire in our car. Eventually someone will cut their finger and eventually we will have a flat. The person who has to have everything go smoothly will have a hard time making progress. Learn to solve problems so you don't have to fear them happening. Expect to start as a beginner and progress from there.

I'm afraid if I set boundaries with my spouse, it will make his (or her) psychological disorder worse.

This is an important concern and there are a few factors to consider before choosing which limits to set. The first limits you set should always be in regard to safety, whether it is yours, your spouse's, or your other family members. Setting these limits may make your spouse's symptoms worse, but also gives your spouse the best chance for treatment. Usually, both happen—the symptoms worsen and treatment commences. The same is true for setting boundaries after your spouse is already receiving treatment. Symptoms may worsen, and then improve as your spouse learns how to deal with your boundaries.

As long as you are setting healthy boundaries and not trying to change everything all at once, you will be helping your spouse to improve. Healthy change is not easy for anyone, mental illness or not. But, it does less damage than maintaining unhealthy conditions. If you will end up leaving your spouse if you don't set boundaries, then you can ask yourself which will be harder for your spouse to cope with—your boundary, or your leaving?

I'm the one with the psychological disorder. How can I use agreement to make things better?

What you will want to avoid is letting your spouse fall into either being your servant or your parent, and you also want to avoid being avoided. To do that, you must educate yourself well about your disorder and understand the difference between your spouse helping you and your spouse being codependent. If your spouse becomes subservient, agree that he or she is very helpful, but also make it clear how being on the same level as you would help you even more.

Do what you can to also care for your spouse. Just because you have a psychological disorder doesn't mean you can't help others. In fact, helping others is one of the healthiest things you can do when you have a psychological disorder. If your spouse starts to become too controlling, supposedly for your sake, agree with the importance of good health, but also set boundaries that allow you to make your own decisions.

I'm not happy and I want to leave my spouse, but it makes me feel guilty. Do you have any advice?

It seems that you have come to the conclusion that the reason you are not happy is because you are with your spouse. If you are right, then most likely you have a relationship problem. Working on that will either improve your relationship or bring both you and your spouse to the point where a divorce makes some sense to the *both* of you.

If you are unhappy but don't have a relationship problem, then I think you have the wrong expectation about relationships. Relationships are for sharing happiness—they aren't for creating happiness. People who expect their partners to make them happy tend to blame their partners any time they are not happy. They give up responsibility and control over their own happiness.

If this is your case, then I recommend working on learning how to take charge of your life and create your own happiness. Doing so may revitalize your relationship with your spouse. Even if it doesn't, it makes sense to learn how to do this before ending your

229

marriage, or else you are likely to have the same problem in your next relationship—after the honeymoon period is over (whether you remarry or not, there is always a honeymoon period in relationships).

My spouse blames me for his (or her) psychological problems. Should I leave him (or her)?

Blaming is a way of escaping responsibility. It takes the focus off the blamer and puts it on someone else. No doubt if you left you would also get blamed for abandoning your spouse. A good way to deal with this is to agree with your spouse that he or she might be right and that you both need to put your heads together to figure out what to do about it. Then lead into problem solving as with other problems in this book. By taking the blame to the next level of "What are we going to do about it?" you actually take away the advantage of blaming. Problem solving is a responsibility taking process. By doing this, either your spouse will participate with you in problem solving and realize how blaming works against him or her; or your spouse will stop blaming you because he or she won't want to do the problem solving. Either way results in a win-win because of the relationship improvement for both of you.

Summary

If neither you nor your spouse have a psychological disorder, it may just be because neither of you has been diagnosed with one by a professional, or that you don't have one *yet*. Psychological disorders are not inevitable, but they are common (especially the mild ones). In a long term relationship, psychological disorders are likely to happen from time to time, just as physical illnesses are. In some relationships, psychological disorders will be chronic.

Psychological disorders don't need to be either the end of your relationship or the end of your happiness. Managing communication with a spouse who has a psychological disorder is in many ways similar to managing communication with a spouse who does not have a psychological disorder. There are a few relationship traps to avoid that can come with either psychological or physical illness. These traps result in a loss of partnership by changing the role of the healthy partner into either a servant or a parent. Unless your spouse is severely incapacitated, such a role shift is unnecessary and actually harmful.

Using the method of agreement, along with good boundaries, can help you to maintain a partnership and loving relationship. One caveat of being able to maintain proper boundaries is the necessity of needing to educate yourself about the nature and treatment of the disorder. Become educated, become an advocate, but stay a partner.

It is important for example, to avoid thinking in terms of finding one, and only one, solution. The term solution too often suggests that somewhere out there is the answer, as if you will fix the entire system in which the problem exists once and only once.

Gerald Nadler & William J Chandon
from *Smart Questions: Learn to Ask the Right Questions for Powerful Results*

♥13♥

WHEN NOT TO AGREE (FOR THE SAKE OF YOUR RELATIONSHIP)

I have shown you in the preceding chapters some of the times for agreement. In this chapter, I will show you some of the times *not* to use the method of agreement. Agreement deepens relationships, but that's not always the best thing. Being aware of how agreement and disagreement affect relationships will help you to more *consciously* decide how you are going to talk to your spouse and others. It is not helpful for us to say whatever comes naturally if what we are saying is contributing to our problems. Our words steer the course of our relationships. Getting better control of them will keep us from going off course.

One of the main reasons that people have trouble rebuilding relationships is that they try to use a single method or single intervention to create change. They search and search and search for the perfect answer to fixing their relationship, find some people who are willing to give single step solutions (such as threatening to divorce or just being patient), and then become very discouraged because they don't have success. This chapter will give you guidance for putting multi-step interventions in the right order. When you finish this chapter, you will have a better understanding of when to use boundaries, when to use agreement, when to use problem solving, and when to walk away.

Know What You Stand For

We have to know what we stand for before we can make a stand. Like most people, I am a person who hates war, but I am not a pacifist. There are times when we must take action which may harm ourselves and harm others as well, in order to prevent a greater injustice or inhumanity. On a large scale, this may mean going to war with another country in order to put an end to genocide. On a small scale, we must sometimes oppose our own family members. For example, to prevent the further abuse of ourselves or our children.

All this is to say that there are times when we must have a focus other than connection and may even need to disconnect. There may be a possibility for connection in the future, just as the United States reconnected with Germany and Japan. But, at the time we take action, our focus is not on the connection because there are more important things at stake.

At times we may have to lose friends, relationships, or even our own lives in the service of a greater good. As the Bible says, "Greater love has no one than this, that he lay down his life for his friends (John 15:13)."

In my limited wisdom I believe there are some things which are clearly wrong. I believe that suicide is wrong. I believe that murder is wrong. I believe that abusing others is wrong. I believe that abusing ourselves is wrong. I believe that allowing others to abuse us or others is wrong. As a marriage and relationship coach, and as a psychologist, I cannot help people to do any of these things and will work to prevent them or end them whenever I can.

You need to decide for yourself what is wrong and what you will not participate in. Although most people would agree with my basic values about what is wrong, there are a very large number of both men and women who are contemplating ending their own lives, who are participating in abuse by direct action or inaction, and who are allowing themselves to be abused. Psychologists are keenly aware of the large number of victims in our society and around the world. Most of us have also experienced or witnessed some kind of victimization in our own families.

In the following sections I want to suggest to you times when you should not agree. I say "should not," because I am using my own value system. You don't have to agree with me, but I hope that you at least can come to a decision about whether you agree or not, and then act in your own life with integrity. Integrity means following our own values, even when it costs us something, or everything, to do that. To lose our integrity is to lose ourselves, to create internal disconnections, which rob us of joy and meaning.

The Right Steps in the Right Order

As you have seen throughout this book, agreement alone will not mend a damaged relationship. Agreement is a necessary precursor to cooperation, which really mends the relationship. But, agreement is not always the first step in the healing process. We must stop the damage before we can heal the wounds. That is why boundaries must come first.

First come boundaries, then agreement, then cooperation. A closer relationship follows. When people continue to have a distant relationship, either they are putting these actions in the wrong order, trying to do them all at once, or are leaving one of them out. If you are continuing to experience problems in your relationship, could it be that you are putting these in the wrong order? Trying to accomplish them all at once? Leaving one of them out?

Boundaries come first because safety comes first

The purpose of boundaries is to stop or prevent harm from being done. They are not something that we do to others. In the physical world there are many boundaries like the barriers that prevent cars from going off the side of a bridge, or the sprinkler systems in buildings that prevent fires from blazing out of control. These barriers are not there to encourage people to drive faster on bridges or to set fires in buildings. They are there because even when we have the best of intentions, accidents still happen.

When there is a dangerous situation, there are two good responses: 1) we can remove the danger; or 2) we can remove ourselves from the dangerous situation. This is true in relationships and other real life situations. If there are gangs where you live, extra police could be brought in, you could hire private security, or you could move away. None of these things will help the gang members. If extra police are brought in, the gang is likely just to move to a different area and victimize someone else. If you hire private security, it will be a continuous expense. And, if you move away, the gang will stay where they are and continue to victimize your old neighbors. But, you will be safe.

Likewise, if you have a dangerous spouse, you can try to get police protection (which often fails), or you can get out and get help. While both of these actions carry risks, they don't carry as much risk as staying with a dangerous person. I would not advise trying to use the method of agreement to end a violent situation. I would recommend the use of boundaries, along with the assistance of professionals, to end the danger. Only when that is done, is it time to consider whether to reconnect or not.

Safety doesn't just mean making sure you aren't killed. It also means making sure that you are not physically injured or threatened. Threats of abuse should always be dealt with as if they were abuse. It make no sense to wait for "actual abuse." You should have zero tolerance for such dangers in your life. If another of your family members is being threatened or physically injured, then help him or her to get help and be safe. And, make sure that you are safe, too. Helping someone else who is being threatened also puts you in harm's way. There are times we must do that, but not recklessly.

My father was a dangerous man. He threatened my mother's life. He abused her, he abused my pets, and he abused me. My mother and I were scared of him. I know what it's like to be in this situation. Unfortunately, my mother did not take action and the result hurt her, my father, and me. My mother did not know what to do, but she could have found out. If you are in such a situation, you may not know what to do either. That is understandable. But, you can find out.

Don't Agree When You Need to Build Respect

The loss of respect in relationships is probably the biggest reason that people fall out of love. It is difficult to feel love toward someone we don't respect, although through self-discipline we can still behave in a loving way. If you don't have your partner's respect, then *earning* that respect will need to come before you work on getting to cooperation through agreement.

How respect is lost

There are various ways to lose respect in a relationship. The fastest way to lose respect is by allowing someone to treat you badly, such as with verbal abuse, physical abuse, or threats. Another way to lose respect is to agree with things that you know are damaging to the relationship. This is why I say throughout this book that although you can use agreement to rebuild from damage done to the relationship, you never agree with the damaging behavior. When the damage is continuing, boundaries must be used to stop the damage. If you agree with a damaging behavior your partner is doing, it becomes apparent that you are either afraid of your partner, or you are afraid of losing your partner. Doing nothing to stop damage, which you are aware of, is also a kind of agreement.

Needing is not the same as loving

The partner who will get the most respect is the one who loves his or her spouse, but who doesn't *need* his or her spouse. The recognition that you could leave if you chose to helps your partner to continue to value you instead of disregard you. My wife is a very capable and attractive woman with a successful career. I know that she could do fine without me and if something were to happen to me or our relationship, she could find a good partner easily. Does that make me feel insecure? No. Quite the contrary, it makes me feel special since she chose to marry me and *wants* to be with me. Likewise I don't *need* her. I would miss her if she left or something happened, but I would be fine. She knows that, too. She knows I am with her because I want to be. I married her because I wanted to. And, we can talk about *anything* because we don't fear rejection. I have never been as close to anyone as I am to her. Love without neediness will let you do that.

Good boundaries are a healthy way of showing your spouse that you are not needy. Refusing to argue also shows you are not needy. You will get respect when you refuse to argue and stick to your boundaries.

Boundaries are not threats and they are not attempts to control someone else's behavior. They are what we do to protect ourselves or others. Two weeks of good boundaries will literally accomplish more than many years of argument. This is proved again and again in my coaching with people who are in high conflict relationships.

Don't Agree When Your Partner's Welfare is at Risk

Taking care of our partner is part of our responsibility, but not in a parental way. Parents need to make decisions for their children. Sometimes, that means they must overrule their children's wishes and actually prevent them from doing things that would be harmful.

Partners though, don't overrule. Not in an equal relationship, anyhow, as is favored in Western cultures. Instead, we tell our partners about our concerns and we refuse to participate in anything that would be harmful to our partner. I don't mean that you refuse to give your partner an ice cream cone because of its high fat, high sugar, content. I mean that you don't help your partner with more severe self-destructive behaviors.

For example, you don't buy alcohol for an alcoholic or cover for him or her by lying to his or her employer. You don't behave like a victim because that would continue to promote your partner being a perpetrator or abuser. You don't refuse to participate with your friends because of your partner's jealousy. And you don't sit around with your depressed partner because that will only contribute more to his or her depression, even though he or she may be comforted by that.

How do you decide when to do what your partner wants, and when to refuse? The same way that you make decisions for yourself—by looking at the long term consequences. So, although agreeing may prevent conflict in the short term, there are times when agreeing will create problems for the long term. Your partner's argument may be that "just one time won't hurt," and although that may be true, every pattern starts with a single action. By all means, if you start to notice a pattern to your behavior or your partner's, and that pattern is destructive, then do not participate in it any more—no matter how much your partner wants you to.

Dislike and danger are two different things

If something your partner wants is not destructive and you merely don't like it, then it might be better to go along with it anyhow. Marriage and committed relationships have to have a certain amount of give and take. If each of you can strive to give more than you take, you will both be better off. If you refuse to give and take, then you will enter into a competition of needs that will destroy your relationship or at least your love for each other. Just think about how many things parents do for their children that they don't want to, or that pet owners do. If we will walk around with our pets picking up their poop every single day, how much more should we be able to do things for our partners at times that we don't really like? Love always has a cost to the person who loves.

Never be abusive with your agreement

Another time not to agree with your partner is when he or she is putting himself or herself down. If your partner says, "I'm so fat, I don't see why you stay with me," then it wouldn't be appropriate to say, "Yes, you are really fat. It's not easy having to look at you each day. " Although it might be agreeing with your partner, it will not connect you. Even in this situation, though, I do not recommend arguing with your partner about it. Simply refuse to participate in it—just as you would refuse to buy alcohol for an alcoholic partner. Reassuring people who put themselves down rewards such behavior with attention. Whenever you see your partner trying to get attention from you in negative ways, make sure you are giving enough attention for positive things instead. You get more of what you pay attention to.

How to Let Your Spouse Know You Don't Agree

Although I want to discourage you from arguing with your partner, I do think that it is important that your partner know why you are not agreeing or going along with his or her behavior. It would be very unnatural for your partner to think, "She doesn't want to be codependent for my problem behavior because it is destructive to me and to our relationship." Instead, he will probably think you are selfish and uncaring.

Giving your partner a loving reason, even if he or she disagrees with your reason, will benefit your relationship. For example, "I'm not going to buy alcohol for you because your alcoholism is causing problems in our relationship and is bad for your body. I want our relationship to be close and I want you to be healthy." To which your partner may respond, "It's MY body. And, it wouldn't cause problems in the relationship if you weren't so hung up about it." Don't argue and don't use the method of agreement because they won't help. You really don't even have to respond at all. Just keep your boundaries and don't explain again. Your partner will replay your reason over and over in his or her mind.

If you do give in to your partner later by buying the alcohol (in this example) he or she will say, "I thought you cared about my body?" To which, you will be at a loss as to what to say and you will lose respect. Your boundaries may anger your partner, but they won't harm your partner. As soon as you do something that harms your partner though, you will lose his or her respect and that will lead to loss of love. It will seem so unfair to you, because you will be doing something your partner wants. To put it another way, if you give candy to your children before dinner, they may thank you at the time and then years later say how much you didn't really care about them. Say "No," when you need to, give a loving reason, and don't argue.

Sometimes Distance Is a Good Thing

I sometimes have an assumption that everyone wants to be as close as possible to their partner. That is true for my clients. There are times though, when a bit of distance is required. Although distance can be created by arguing, arguing can also be damaging and can get out of control if people are very upset. Let's consider a few situations when it might be desirable to have a little distance, and how we can prevent the damage that could be done by arguing.

Intentionally not agreeing, in order to prevent a deep connection with someone

For people who have the skills that my advanced clients and I have, it is possible to create deep and strong feelings of love in someone when it is not appropriate or desirable. It is quite possible to use great relationship skills that the other person has never experienced before and to trigger their "in love" switches, whether you desire that or not. By intentionally not agreeing (not the same as disagreeing), the relationship can be moderated or taken back a notch. Consistent lack of agreement will create easy distance. Consider the following exchange:

Example of "accidentally" deepening a relationship:

> *OPPOSITE SEX COWORKER: "I really have a hard time understanding why people can't be more open and honest with each other."*
> *YOU: "I know what you mean. When we are open and vulnerable with someone we trust it feels so good."*

That kind of agreement deepens the relationship and for a skilled person it slips out as easily as disagreement does for an unskilled person. Mindlessly agreeing is sometimes as bad as mindlessly disagreeing. Let's consider the same example again, with a different reply.

Example of maintaining safe emotional distance:

*OPPOSITE SEX COWORKER: "I really have a
hard time understanding why people can't
be more open and honest with each other."
YOU: "Well, you know it takes time to be
able to trust people."*

This response is not argumentative, but it is not agreeable either. Another thing is that it is honest. If someone you like as a friend is becoming too close, this is a gentle way of backing them off. If it's someone you don't like or someone who is really dense, then you might step up your responses to downright disagreement. Each consecutive disagreement should move you emotionally further and further apart. Regulating the distance in relationships is not manipulation. It is part of taking care of yourself and other people. There is no reason to be dishonest in your interactions. Just put the emphasis where it will do the most good.

Part of the reason that people disagree more easily than they agree may have to do with this function of keeping a safe emotional distance from others. Unfortunately, it has carried over into intimate and familial relationships which should be safe and close. You can consciously and intentionally use disagreement to stay safe where you need to, and agreement to get closer when you want to. It's as important as being able to say both "yes," and "no."

Intentionally not agreeing, in order to maintain a professional distance

Nobody solicits unwanted advances or harassment, but some people unwittingly encourage it. Since agreement tends to be the opposite of rejection, it can send the signal to the advancer that he or she is doing good and to keep coming on to you. In this case I am not talking about a man or woman trying to pick you up in a bar or your next door neighbor. I am talking about someone you need to maintain a working relationship with.

Example exchange between a male supervisor/manager and a female employee:

> *SUPERVISOR/MANAGER: "I realized that I don't mind working overtime because it gives me more of a chance to spend time with you."*
>
> *EMPLOYEE: "I like working with you, too."*

This response by the employee is giving a "green light" to the manager, although it is merely a friendly response. If you were certain that your boss was not coming on to you, it might be ok, too. But...

Here's another way to deal with it that helps to maintain a stronger boundary:

> *SUPERVISOR/MANAGER: "I realized that I don't mind working overtime because it gives me more of a chance to spend time with you."*
>
> *EMPLOYEE: "Is that right? Well, I'd rather be home with my husband."*

You can reverse the genders of these two people. It works the same. My point is that agreement stimulates attraction. People like the people who agree with them. Just because you have a heater doesn't mean you have to turn it on full blast. Moderate your relationships in a way that is good for you and for them. Don't heat everyone up.

Agreement with People Who Enjoy Debate

There are a lot of people who debate, especially in Western culture. Few people actually enjoy it, though. Most are just debating to try to get you to agree with them. Once you do, they stop debating. A small percentage like debate as a communication style. If you agree with them, they will find something new to debate about. If you keep agreeing with them, they will be so turned off that they won't want anything to do with you. It's just like joking with a joker makes them joke more. Always being serious with a joker will make them joke with someone else.

People who like to debate are usually intellectuals, verbal, and creative. While you are saying something, they are thinking of the exceptions to what you are saying. Then, they will say, "What about ...(exception 1, exception 2, etc.). It's not that they are trying to fight with you or to prove you wrong. It's more like they are trying to show off how smart they are. If you get two such people together, while the first one is saying, "What about... (exception 1, exception 2, etc.)," the other one is saying, "that's true." But, unlike an argument where each person will continue to defend their perspective, they will then move on to a related subject or another subject altogether. I occasionally like to talk with such people, but it can get rather tiring.

If you want to end debate with such people, you can simply start using the agreement method, without noting any exceptions or other perspectives. They will then quickly tire of trying to debate you. As long as you argue (debate), they will continue. You can end up feeling like you have just played a chess tournament.

There is an advantage to having a group of people who like to debate rather than agree. They can come up with a variety of creative possibilities. The business applications are endless. The solutions they choose are likely to be well thought out. On the other hand, if you get a group of people together who just agree with each other, creativity is stifled. This has been a problem in Japanese industry for many years since Japanese culturally favor agreement and shun disagreement. Some people credit the great number of inventions that have come out of the United States with American's tendency to consider differences rather than similarities. In this book, I have shown you that the best time to consider differences is in the problem solving process, and not before. Then you and your spouse can come up with creative possibilities for your relationship.

Summary

Agreement is most useful in close relationships to build strong connections and to deepen intimacy. But we must be careful not to agree when what we are agreeing with is harmful to ourselves or others. When there is a lot of damage in a relationship, multiple steps will be required to fix it.

Because safety must come first, agreement cannot come first in relationships which have ongoing damage or dangers. In such cases, boundaries must come first. If the boundaries do not succeed, then agreement may never be possible. Effort must be put into boundaries therefore, or your relationship will end.

With people outside of our family and friends it may be more important to regulate distance than to promote closeness. The method of agreement is a powerful way of communication that can pull people in too close. In some instances, a little disagreement may be helpful.

The difference between the right word and the almost right word is the difference between lightning and a lightning bug.

Mark Twain
US Humorist & Author

EPILOGUE

Well, what did you think of the information in this book? My hope is that it was not *merely* interesting or intriguing. I wrote this book to give you something practical and helpful to do. If you haven't tried to use agreement and continue to argue or avoid, then I won't take responsibility for that. You will either decide to put the material to use or not, either now or in the future. At least you have the information on hand. I will caution you though, not to wait too long before trying new things if what you are doing now is not working. Time is never on your side in a troubled relationship. Rather than healing all wounds, time tends to cement differences.

If Things Are Not Improving

If you have used the information in this book and haven't had improvement in your relationship, then I have failed you somehow, and I apologize. These ways do work for most people and for most situations, but sometimes more is needed. No method is foolproof and there are many ways for things to go wrong.

Using the method of agreement is a skill, and like all skills, it improves with success. Skills don't improve merely as a result of learning and practice, although learning and practice are both required. For skills to develop there must also be some success, even the tiniest amount. That tiny success then becomes the seed from which all other successes will grow.

In my job as a marriage and relationship coach, I help people to have success. Sometimes their first success is in healthy communication. I also help them to help their partners to have success with them. In my opinion, there is no way to improve a relationship without looking for win-win solutions. The problem solving method in this book is one example of how to create a win-win. Relationships do take two, so people must help their spouses to have success with them. Even so, It is possible to do everything right and for a relationship to fail, especially if a spouse has totally lost interest in the relationship.

I have attempted with this book to help you to have a little success and to show you how to help your spouse to have a little success with you. From there, growth is possible. From there, growth is desirable. And from there, growth means the two of you becoming closer—maybe even getting all the way to Oneness.

A Review of Relationship Improvement Principles

There are three major principles that I have consistently presented throughout this book. They are about disconnection, connection, and boundaries. The better you understand these three principles, the better relationships you will have when you *deliberately* apply communication methods. If you simply rely on habit and do not apply these principles, then you will end up where you started. By living consciously and deliberately, you can have the kind of life and relationships that you want to have.

We create our own distance in relationships

It is not only what our partners do that can create distance in our relationships, it is also how we respond to what our partners do (or don't do). Many people overly focus on the actions of their partners, which they can't directly control. When we do this, we become powerless and feel like victims, trapped in never-ending bad relationships. If we instead focus on our reactions to what our partners are doing, we become empowered. We can make changes in the way we respond, which in turn changes the way our partners treat us.

There are a variety of ways to respond to our partners which are common and understandable, but *not* helpful. When we respond with verbal disagreement and argument, no matter how right we are, it adds to the distance without solving any problems. When we fail to use boundaries to stop ongoing damaging behaviors, we also contribute to the damage. When we set good boundaries, but fail to use loving messages, we create still more distance. And when we respond with avoidance, we are neither being patient nor being loving. The longer we avoid taking actions which could help others, our partner, or ourselves, the more *we* are responsible for the results.

These are lessons that Jesus taught 2000 years ago. We *are* responsible for our neighbor. Faith without action is dead, and love without helping is no love at all. These ideas may be somewhat radical for people who believe that all responsibility lies with the person who is behaving badly. But, it is also empowering because it means that improving relationships does not depend on waiting for a problem spouse or significant other to shape up on his or her own.

Agreeing is strength, not weakness

Agreement builds connection in a way that is really hard for other people to resist. How can we fight people who agree with us? If your spouse, parent, friends, or others fight against you, agreeing with them is a sure route to ending the fighting. It is one of the best kept secrets of modern society that we win more when we agree than when we disagree. Somehow the meaning of agreement has been twisted to mean being submissive. If anything, the method of agreement helps you to be more powerful.

When I suggest to someone that they agree with their spouse in order to build connection, they often react right away against how submissive that feels. In actuality, you will find that instead of being submissive, agreement makes you strong, secure, and effective. On the other hand, arguing will make you weak, ineffective, and insecure. The more you argue, the more you are likely to lose your relationship. Agreement puts you in a position to be both influential and loving; disagreement puts you in a position to have no influence at all, while rapidly losing love and respect. All you have to do is try them both out to discover the truth of this.

Submission is not a bad thing

Although agreement is not the same as submission, that does not mean that submission is bad. Submission really has to do with letting someone use power to control you. That in itself is neither good nor bad. It really depends on what they have us do. Children submit to their parents who may either harm them or help them. So we also do with teachers, leaders, employers, police, military commanders, and yes, even spouses. What do I believe about submitting to spouses? I believe that wives *and* husbands will benefit from submitting themselves to each other when each uses his or her power to build the relationship.

Allowing your spouse to harm you or the relationship is *not* submission; it is negligence. It hurts him (or her) as well as you. There is nothing loving in allowing yourself to be abused or the relationship to be damaged. In times like this, you need a method for stopping the damage without being vengeful. That method is expressing love while having good boundaries.

Boundaries are an expression of love

Boundaries are often misunderstood to be something that we do *against* our partner or something that we try to get our partner to do. But, as you have seen in this book, boundaries are actions that *we* take to prevent further harm to the relationship. When we do that, we are helping ourselves as well as our spouses. Small boundaries are needed for daily irritations that eat away at our relationships, and big boundaries are needed when there are more serious dangers.

We communicate our boundaries and help our spouses to understand that our boundaries are being done out of our love for them. We don't expect them to understand or appreciate that at first. If our boundaries are good ones, and if we continue to connect lovingly in other ways, our boundaries earn us respect and help our partner to feel secure in our love. As the Bible says, we are to "Speak the truth in love (Ephesians 4:15a)." That doesn't mean that every word that comes out of our mouth will be loving, but that what we say needs to be motivated by love. Telling your child that he can't have candy just before dinner is loving, no matter how much he hates it. So is telling your spouse that you will immediately leave, for a time, if he verbally abuses you. Women who say this and follow through go on to have respect from their husbands and much better marriages. Those who simply complain or ignore such abuse, without setting boundaries, have worse marriages. Good boundaries are an expression of our love and desire to have a close relationship. It's part of what being a good partner means.

Connection Is Not Enough

Couples need a method for dealing with life intrusions as they happen. I think it is *mostly* the young and inexperienced who believe that if they love each other enough, then they won't have problems. Life does not allow for the uninterrupted smooth continuation of anything. Even diamonds—one of the hardest substances in the universe—eventually will wear away to dust. Relationships are closer to marshmallows in durability than to diamonds. They are subject to many kinds of destruction and require daily maintenance. What's more, a problem fixed is not a problem fixed forever. A relationship can't simply be polished up once a year.

In this book, I have given you just one of the methods for cooperatively fixing problems in a relationship as you go along. I have called it "problem solving," but in actuality, it is just one of many ways of doing problem solving. I chose to give you the method I did because it is easy to learn, easy to initiate, and can be used for a wide variety of situations. It is the Swiss army knife of problem solving. You can use it almost anywhere, almost anytime, with almost anyone.

It is possible though, that you have used the method of agreement as set out in this book, combined it with good boundaries, worked together with your spouse using problem solving, and still ended up avoiding each other. When that happens, it isn't time to give up or fall back on some previous way of problem solving (they also didn't work or you wouldn't be where you are now); it will be time to try something different.

Radio in Before Bailing Out

Have you ever seen any of those old TV movies about an airplane that has some kind of engine problem and the pilots have all somehow been incapacitated? That feeling of doom and panic that the passengers have can also be experienced in problem relationships. It sounds like an exaggeration, I know, but there are many people who panic when they discover their spouse having an affair, their spouse filing for divorce, they find drugs rolled up in their spouse's sock, or many other situations. All of these things on a physical level feel like being kicked in the gut. It's easy to panic.

When you are overwhelmed, have taken an emotional kick to the gut, and don't know what to do, it is time to call for help. That's what the people (usually a flight attendant) did in those airline disaster movies. They radioed the tower at the airport for help. The tower got an expert on the radio, and the expert talked the flight attendant through each step of what to do to bring the plane to a safe landing (hopefully—with breath held, and fingers crossed). After a safe, but scary landing, everyone hugged and kissed and were happy to be alive. The guys in the tower didn't hug and kiss, but just went on to help the next plane, which is the way it should be.

My job is to be in the tower and to take those calls. I need to be prepared by knowing what to do in your situation and be able to talk you through it as soon as you call. I can't do any of the things that you have to do for you, but I can save you from frantically having to look through the manual and trying to fly safely at the same time. When serious problems happen, time is never on our side. My specialty is helping people who have run out of ideas on how to fix their relationship. Because they can think of no way, they often believe there is no way and bail out. People who come to me have often run out of ideas, but still have hope that there might be a way. Almost always, there is.

One More Word of Encouragement

Some of my clients are other coaches and therapists. There are times when even the experts can't help themselves. They don't feel ashamed about it and neither should you. You are not expected to know everything, even if you are an expert. You are only expected to do what you can and then to get help with the rest. For me, knowing that really helps me to take it easier on myself. I hope it does for you, too.

Thank You

Thank you for reading this book. I would love to hear from you. You can find my contact information in the "About the Author" section.

Far better is it to dare mighty things, to win glorious triumphs, even though checkered by failure , than to take rank with those poor spires who neither enjoy much nor suffer much because they live in the gray twilight that knows not victory or defeat.

Theodore Roosevelt
26th President of the US

ABOUT THE AUTHOR

Coach Jack is no stranger to family conflict. His own personal hell started when he was five years old. His earliest memories are of hiding under his bed with his hands pressed to his ears while his parents fought. He was scared. Scared for his mother and scared for himself. His father had proved over and over again that there was good reason to be.

Part of Coach Jack's own healing was making his past more meaningful by helping couples to be able to overcome conflict. To not merely endure their situation, but to improve it. Coach Jack's mother didn't know how to do that. She wanted to divorce, but she was afraid that she wouldn't be able to make it on her own. Many variations of this situation are occurring in our society. With help like Coach Jack provides, men and women are learning how to love and help each other—to live as One. He would say that the biggest shame is not that people are divorcing, but that they are unnecessarily hurting each other in their efforts to be loved.

We could say that now Coach Jack does marriage and relationship coaching and helps people save their relationships, but that doesn't really tell you what he does. What he really does is:

- help people feel capable of handling their problems
- help people to stop their partners from doing things which damage relationships
- help people to feel important to their partner
- help people to look forward to their day
- help people to enjoy going to bed with their partner
- help couples to be able to share their thoughts and feelings and to laugh together
- help people to enjoy giving and receiving help from their partner
- help people to be glad to see their partner
- help people to have a happier home
- help people to have happier children (by improving their relationship)

What Coach Jack would tell you from his experiences is that it is all very doable. For couples who do not want to divorce, there is always a way to improve their relationship. Coach Jack believes that when people run out of options, it is not time to give up, but time to get more options. Although he recognizes that divorces sometimes happen, and may need to happen, they are always sad. He would tell you that as a marriage and relationship coach, it is not his place to recommend divorce, but simply to do all that he can to help.

To update you on his life, Coach Jack has two sons who are in college and doing well. His wife is a marriage counselor for Japanese people. Coach Jack took his wife's family name when they married; that's how he became an "Ito" (originally he's from Vermont). His wife is his best friend, his lover, and helper—a true partner. One of Coach Jack's personal goals is to make her laugh every day.

Coach Jack's practice includes people from many countries, cultures, and religions. He gets email from all over the world and tries to respond personally to everyone.

You are welcome to write to Coach Jack or to visit his blog for more helpful information on a variety of relationship problems.

Contact Information:

email: coachjack@coachjackito.com
Skype: jack.ito

Website:

coachjackito.com

Abbreviated Biography

Birthplace: Vermont, USA

1985 Bachelor of Arts in Psychology, St. Michael's College, Colchester, Vermont

1988 Master of Arts in Psychology, East Tennessee State University, Johnson City, Tennessee

1993 Master of Arts in Theology, Fuller Theological Seminary, Graduate School of Theology, Pasadena, California

1994 Doctor of Philosophy in Clinical Psychology, Fuller Theological Seminary, Graduate School of Psychology, Pasadena, California

Undergraduate and Graduate Professor of Psychology at Geneva College, Beaver Falls, Pennsylvania

Director Olive Branch Counseling Services, Chippewa, Pennsylvania

Post Traumatic Stress Specialist, United States Navy, Bremerton, Washington, and 29 Palms, California

Graduate MentorCoach Certified Coaching Program

Books: What to Do When He Won't Change (2011)

Coaching Specialties: Fostering Intimacy in Severely Damaged Marriages and Committed Relationships

Coaching Venues: Individuals and Couples

Whatever you are, be a good one.

Abraham Lincoln
16th President of the US

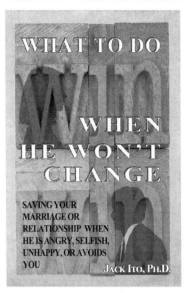

What to Do When He Won't Change

Saving Your Marriage or Relationship When He Is Angry, Selfish, Unhappy, or Avoids You

(2011) 249 pages

Has your partner become an angry, selfish, unhappy, or avoidant person? Does he refuse to go to counseling or work on your relationship? Would you like a way to make things better without having to end your relationship or threaten to?

In *What To Do When He Won't Change*, you will learn the four major motivations that drive men's behavior in relationships. You can then use the down to earth examples and win-win interventions to work with your partner's motivations rather than against them. The result? Faster change with less conflict.

Available at online bookstores in paperback or as a downloadable Kindle eBook from Amazon.com

Little by little, one travels far.

J. R. R. Tolkien
British Scholar & Author

INDEX

D

E

F

Made in the USA
Middletown, DE
17 January 2016